Ground Covers in the Landscape

Emile L. Labadie

illustrations by
Jane S. Andrews

Sierra City Press   1983

by the same author:

Native Plants for use in the California Landscape
Ornamental Shrubs for use in the Western Landscape

Copyright©1982 by Emile L. Labadie
All rights reserved under International and
Pan American Copyright Conventions.
FIRST EDITION
Library of Congress Catalog Card No. 82-099919
International Standard Book Number:
            0-9604160-5-6 cloth
            0-9604160-4-8 paper
Designed by Evelyn Labadie and Jane Andrews
No part of this work covered by the copyrights
hereon may be reproduced or used in any form or
by any means - graphic, electronic, or mechanical,
including photocopying, recording, taping, or
information storage and retrieval systems -
without written permission of the publisher.
Printed and bound by Edwards Brothers,
            Ann Arbor, Michigan.
Manufactured in the United States of America.
Published and distributed by Sierra City Press,
            P.O. Box 2, Sierra City, California 96125
10 9 8 7 6 5 4 3 2 1
Cover illustration by Jane Andrews.
  Heterocentron elegans
Back cover photograph by James Fajardo

TABLE OF CONTENTS

PREFACE

This book is dedicated to my family whom I love dearly; to my wife Evelyn, to my sons Emile, Dean, Bruce and Craig, to my daughters Denise and Cheri and to all of their loved ones.

I wrote this book for horticulture students, young and old, but especially for the young ones, because it is they who have the energy and the idealism to take up a challenge and to make this a better, more beautiful world.

Horticulture students are an especially favorite group of mine, for it is they who are already interested in plants and who are eager to know more about them and their uses in the landscape and elsewhere. Theirs is a fascinating field. There is so much to learn that they will never learn it all, and yet for that reason, they will have to, and will want to, continue their education year after year.

And to those professional organizations that encourage young horticulturists to further their education, I say well done! Among these concerned groups I include, from personal experience, the California Association of Nurserymen, the California Landscape Contractors Association and the Northern California Turfgrass Council.

These organizations provide scholarships for students so that they can pursue their goals in horticulture. In addition, they often recognize the efforts of educators who direct these young people in the educational process. These educators, and I am not talking about administrators, but rather about those dedicated, over-burdened and grossly underpaid teachers without whom the whole educational system would completely collapse. It is these teachers who need this recognition and support and who truly deserve it.

1

I must thank my dear wife Evelyn, for all that she has done and continues to do, to make this book a reality. I want to thank Jane Andrews for her illustrations, beautiful and accurate to the finest detail, all from observations in the field throughout the seasons.

Finally, to Carl M. Muecke who supervised the typesetting and layout, while at the same time going in many directions, and to Julie Arnold who did the actual typesetting, I express my gratitude for a professional job.

Emile L. Labadie
Horticultural Consultant,
Emeritus Professor of Ornamental Horticulture
Merritt College

Oakland, California
June 1, 1983

INTRODUCTION

Perhaps the ideal ground cover is turfgrass. If it is managed properly - mowed at the correct height depending on the genus and species, fertilized regularly and watered systematically, it may form a green carpet very pleasing to the eye.

Grass, however, is a high-maintenance type of landscaping. And even though it is usually more tolerant to traffic than other plants, still something may be desired that requires less effort to maintain.

Low-growing plants other than grass may be an alternative. Plants that grow up to a height of from several inches to 3 feet and that spread over the soil area are considered to be ground covers. Certain ones that may reach a greater height but that have a spreading effect might still be placed in the ground cover category.

Some of these plants may furnish color other than just green. The foliage itself may be variegated. Some may have very distinctive flowers and some may have colorful fruit. Some may have all of these characteristics.

Ground covers may have very different habits. Some may be prostrate on the soil area. Others may be upright. Some may be sprawling. Whatever the habit, these plants can be used to create various pleasant effects in the landscape.

Before using any plant in the landscape, one should be aware of the plant characteristics. How rapidly is it going to spread. How long will it last before having to be replaced. What problems is it going to present. Is it going to be too aggressive and/or invasive. Is it a plant that attracts bees. Is it a common host for insects and diseases. Answers to all of these questions should be available before planting.

It should be noted also, that certain ground covers as Ivy and Star Jasmine, for example, provided refuge for rodents such as mice and rats. These creatures can easily move out from their cover, to forage on choice nearby plants - or, they may even work their way into an adjacent residence or other structure.

Ground covers can perform an important function in any landscape. They should be chosen carefully so that they do not become a maintenance nightmare. If a plant is described as being widespread, aggressive and invasive, be sure that it fits your particular need before you plant it. Some of the ground covers should not be placed into the landscape unless they are in contained areas such as parking strips or concrete boxes.

Proper soil preparation is very important. The type of soil, the structure, the drainage - all may affect the ultimate success or failure of any particular planting. Most soils can be improved with the addition of soil amendments. These can be incorporated into the soil to improve the structure. Organic matter of all kinds can usually be used. This would include compost, leaf mold, peat moss and sawdust. An excess of organics might require the addition of nitrogen.

Certain plants need more light than others, so one should be familiar with the particular plant requirements. Some plants are more tolerant to or do better in shade. Others might be tolerant to or do best in a sunny location. Some prefer a moist soil. Others might do very well in a dry situation.

Before planting, weeds should be eliminated. This is usually much easier to accomplish prior to planting. In the case of persistent weeds such as Bermuda Grass, the soil might have to be fumigated in order to achieve satisfactory control.

Some thought should be given to using a mulch between plants, either for aesthetic purposes or for the control of weeds until the plants can cover a particular area.

An efficient irrigation system is important, as is a program for applying the necessary nutrients. The species of plant will determine the amount of water needed and the frequency. Many plants will benefit from periodic fertilizing. The method of application must be determined according to the type of ground cover. In some cases, broadcasting of a dry commercial fertilizer will be effective, if watered in thoroughly following application. In other cases, plants might be injured and one might have to apply liquid formulations.

As for pruning, some ground covers can be cut severely, even with a mower, while others will look best when trimmed moderately. Still others may require very little or no pruning.

When plants are well-established, they may be quite drought-tolerant. Also, when they are growing in some shade, they may be more tolerant to a dry situation than when in full sun.

Only those plants that are broadleafs are discussed in this book. Most of these are exotic in that they originate in many parts of the world. A few are from North America, but California native plants are not included.

The lists compiled relative to plants for particular situations are arbitrary. In areas other than the west, the plants in the lists might vary somewhat. In order for students and others to identify various ground covers, I have compiled keys. For those of you who prefer not to use a key, you can thumb through the pages until, hopefully, you find the particular plant that you might be looking for. You will find the illustrations quite accurate, being drawn to scale and showing leaf, flower and fruit in detail.

Authorities for the nomenclature used in this book include *Hortus Third* and *An Annotated Checklist of Woody Ornamental Plants of California, Oregon and Washington*. Where these differ, I have usually used the latter reference because it is the more recent.

DESCRIPTION of PLANT PARTS

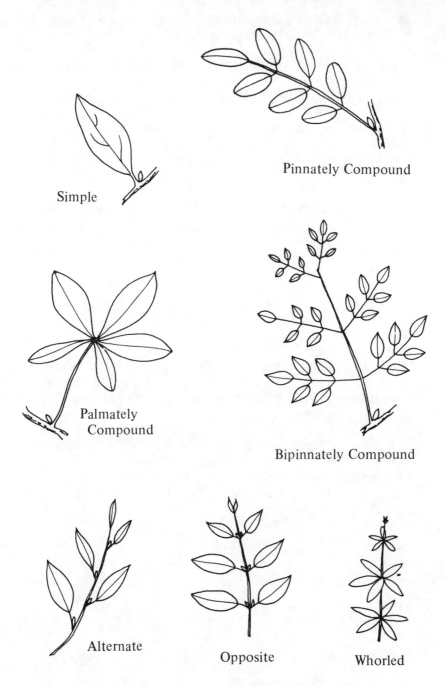

Simple

Pinnately Compound

Palmately
Compound

Bipinnately Compound

Alternate

Opposite

Whorled

LEAF ARRANGEMENTS

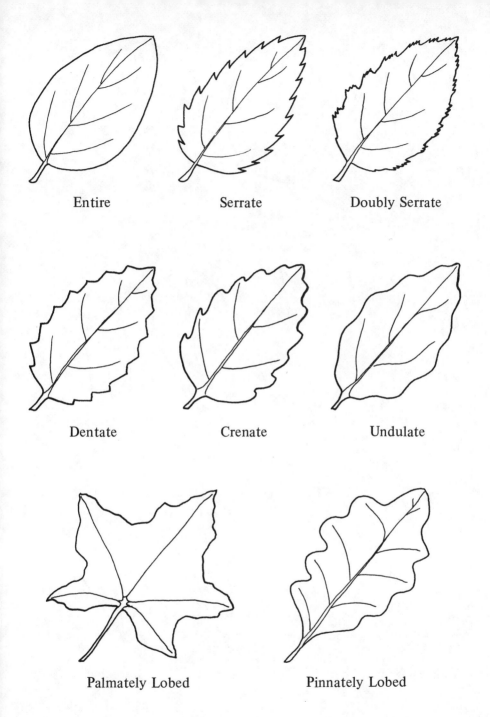

Entire   Serrate   Doubly Serrate

Dentate   Crenate   Undulate

Palmately Lobed   Pinnately Lobed

LEAF MARGINS

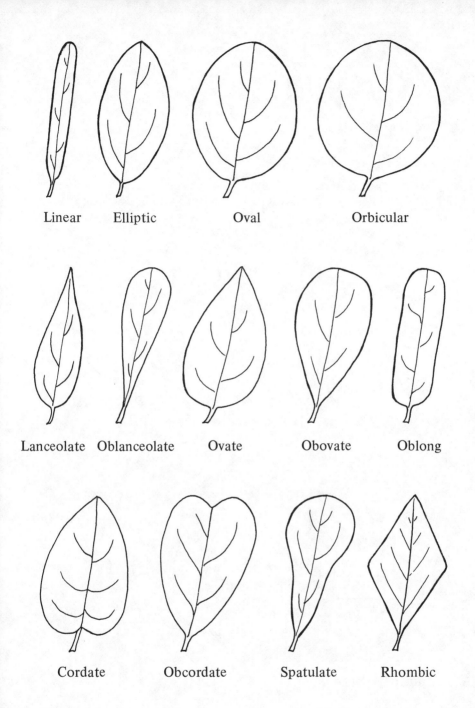

Linear Elliptic Oval Orbicular

Lanceolate Oblanceolate Ovate Obovate Oblong

Cordate Obcordate Spatulate Rhombic

LEAF SHAPES

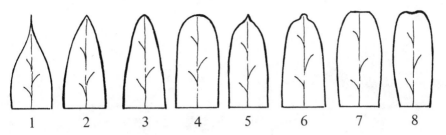

1. Acuminate   2. Acute   3. Obtuse   4. Rounded   5. Cuspidate
6. Mucronate   7. Truncate   8. Emarginate

LEAF APEXES

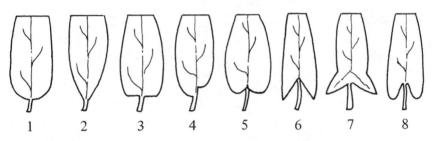

1. Rounded   2. Cuneate   3. Truncate   4. Oblique   5. Cordate
6. Sagittate   7. Hastate   8. Auriculate

LEAF BASES

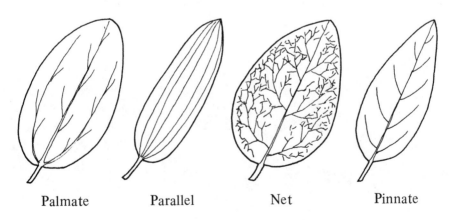

Palmate   Parallel   Net   Pinnate

LEAF VENATION

FLOWERS

Regular

Irregular

FLOWER PARTS

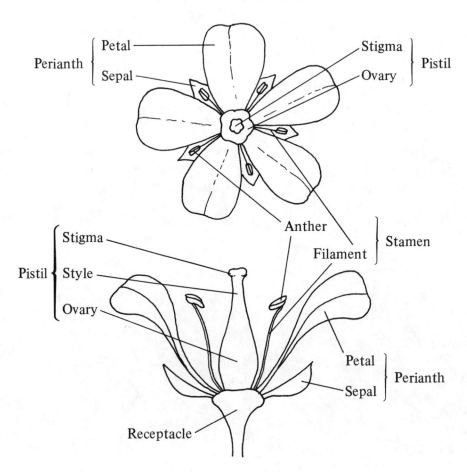

Perianth { Petal
           Sepal

Stigma } Pistil
Ovary

Anther] Stamen
Filament

Pistil { Stigma
         Style
         Ovary

Petal] Perianth
Sepal

Receptacle

TYPES OF INFLORESCENCES

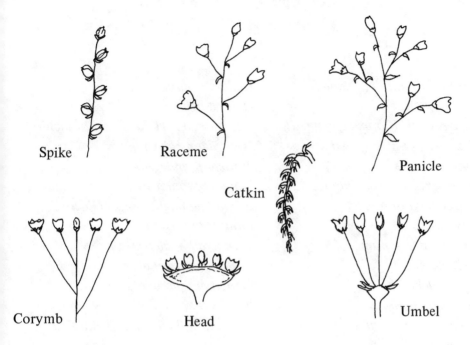

Spike

Raceme

Catkin

Panicle

Corymb

Head

Umbel

TYPES OF FRUIT

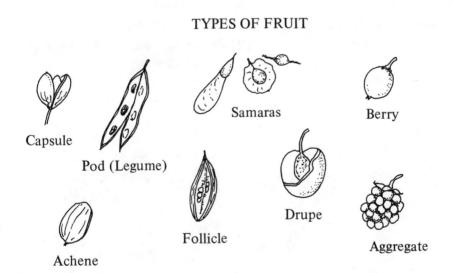

Capsule

Pod (Legume)

Samaras

Berry

Achene

Follicle

Drupe

Aggregate

12

Woody Ground Cover Plants

Andromeda polifolia 'Nana'
Ardisia japonica
Asparagus densiflorus 'Sprengeri'
Berberis stenophylla 'Irwinii'
Calluna vulgaris
Ceratostigma plumbaginoides
Chorizema cordatum
Cistus salvifolius
Convolvulus cneorum
Coprosma kirkii
Correa pulchella
Cotoneaster dammeri
Cotoneaster horizontalis
Cotoneaster microphyllus
Daphne cneorum
Erica herbacea 'Springwood White'
Euonymus fortunei var. radicans
Gardenia augusta 'Radicans'
Gaultheria procumbens
Grevillea 'Noell'
Grewia occidentalis

Hedera canariensis
Hedera helix
Hedera helix 'Hahn's Self-Branching'
Hypericum calycinum
Justicia brandegeana
Lantana montevidensis
Lavandula angustifolia 'Hidcote'
Lithodora diffusa
Loropetalum chinense
Pelargonium peltatum
Pernettya mucronata
Prunus laurocerasus 'Zabeliana'
Pyracantha koidzumi 'Santa Cruz'
Rosmarinus officinalis 'Prostratus'
Santolina chamaecyparissus
Sarcococca hookerana var. humilis
Senecio cineraria
Sollya heterophylla
Trachelospermum jasminoides
Viburnum davidii

Key to Woody Ground Cover Plants

A - **Leaves bluish-gray, grayish or whitish**
  B - **Leaves aromatic**
    Leaves alternate   *Santolina chamaecyparissus, p. 234*
    Leaves opposite
      Flowers white   *Cistus salvifolius, p. 80*
      Flowers lavender
        Inflorescence 6 to 10-flowered and to 3 inches long
                          Lavandula angustifolia
                              'Hidcote' , *p. 184*
        Inflorescence in short, axillary racemes
                          Rosmarinus officinalis
                            'Prostratus' , *p. 230*
  BB - **Leaves not aromatic**
    Leaves pinnately lobed   *Senecio cineraria, p. 248*
    Leaves not pinnately lobed
    Leaves opposite   *Correa pulchella, p. 92*
    Leaves alternate
      Leaves glabrous both sides   *Andromeda*
      Leaves not as above   *polifolia 'Nana', p. 38*
        Leaves white tomentose both sides. Flowers white.
                    Convolvulus cneorum, p. 84
        Leaves not as above. Flowers a brilliant blue.
                    Lithodora diffusa, p. 188

AA - **Leaves not commonly bluish-gray, grayish or whitish**
  B - **Leaves alternate**
    C - **Leaves aromatic**   *Gaultheria procumbens, p. 136*
    CC - **Leaves not aromatic**
      D - **Leaves palmately lobed**
      Flowers may be of various colors. Fruit shaped as
        a stork's bill   *Pelargonium peltatum, p. 210*
      Flowers and fruit not as above
      Leaves to 6 inches across and as long
                    Hedera canariensis, p. 152
      Leaves mostly not as long nor as wide as the above
      Leaves 2 to 3 inches long and to 1½ inches
        wide
          Lobes often more acute than with the other
            2 Hederas   *Hedera helix 'Hahn's*
                      Self-Branching' , *p. 156*
         Leaves larger than the above and usually a
          darker green   *Hedera helix, p. 154*

DD - **Leaves pinnately lobed**
    Leaves prickly. Stems with   *Berberis stenophylla*
      3-parted spines   *'Irwinii'* ,   *p. 56*
DDD - **Leaves not pinnately lobed**
    E - **Leaves toothed**
        Leaves to 4 or 5 inches long
          Inflorescence an ascending raceme, to 1 1/4 inches
                                      Prunus laurocerasus
                                  'Zabeliana',   *p. 226*
          Inflorescence not as above   *Ardisia japonica, p. 46*
        Leaves 2 1/2 to 3 inches long
          Flowers lavender   *Grewia occidentalis, p. 148*
          Flowers white. Stems spinose   *Pyracantha koidzumi*
                                 'Santa Cruz' ,   *p. 228*
        Leaves to one inch or less in length
          Flowers orange-red   *Chorizema cordatum, p. 78*
          Flowers white to pink   *Pernettya mucronata, p. 214*
  EE - **Leaves entire**
    F - **Leaves needlelike**
        Flowers white to pink. Regular. *Asparagus densiflorus*
        Fruit red. Stems spinose   *'Sprengeri'* ,   *p. 50*

        Flowers white to pink. Irregular. Stems and fruit not as
        above.   *Grevillea 'Noell', p. 146*

    FF - **Leaves not needlelike**
      G - Flowers blue
          Flowers campanulate. Pendulous. Plant spread
            and height 5 to 6 feet   *Sollya heterophylla, p. 252*
          Flowers salverform. In dense heads. Plant
            height 6 to 15 inches. Widespread
                    Ceratostigma plumbaginoides, p. 72
      GG - Flowers pink, fading to white
                 Andromeda polifolia 'Nana', p. 38
    GGG - Flowers white
      H - **Flowers especially fragrant**
        Leaves to 3 inches long, 3/4 inch wide.
          Fruit dark   *Sarcococca hookerana*
                         var. humilis ,   *p. 236*
        Leaves to one inch long, 1/4 inch wide.
          Fruit not as above. Flowers white to pink
                     Daphne cneorum, p. 104

HH - Flowers not especially fragrant
Leaves to 2 inches long, to one inch wide.
Flowers in terminal clusters
Loropetalum chinense, p. 190
Leaves shorters than the above and usually
not over 1/2 inch wide
Leaves white or grayish-hairy below
Plant 3 to 6 inches high
Cotoneaster dammeri, p. 94
Plant 2 to 3 feet high
Cotoneaster microphyllus, p. 98
Leaves not as above
Cotoneaster horizontalis, p. 96

BB - Leaves opposite
C - Leaves toothed
Leaves aromatic *Lantana montevidensis, p. 180*
Leaves not aromatic
Leaves to 6 inches long *Viburnum davidii, p. 268*
Leaves one to 2 inches long *Euonymus fortunei
var. radicans, p. 122*
CC - Leaves entire
Flowers yellow *Hypericum calycinum, p. 170*
Flowers pink *Calluna vulgaris, p. 60*
Flowers white or whitish
Leaves 2-ranked, needlelike or awl-shaped
*Erica herbacea
'Springwood White', p. 114*

Leaves not as above

Flowers very fragrant
Leaves exuding a whitish substance when injured. Flower
petals arranged in pinwheel fashion
Trachelospermum jasminoides, p. 260
Leaves and flowers not as above
Gardenia augusta 'Radicans', p. 134
Flowers not noticeably fragrant
Flowers irregular. In pendulous spikes to 6 inches
in length. With conspicuous bracts
Justicia brandegeana, p. 176
Flowers regular. Funnelform. Solitary or in cymes
Coprosma kirkii, p. 88

Herbaceous Ground Cover Plants

Acanthus mollis

Achillea ageratifolia

Achillea tomentosa

Agapanthus orientalis

Agapanthus orientalis 'Peter Pan'

Ajuga reptans

Arabis caucasica

Arcthotheca calendula

Armeria maritima

Aubrieta deltoidea

Aurinia saxatilis

Bergenia crassifolia

Campanula portenschlagiana

Campanula poscharskyana

Carpobrotus edulis

Centranthus ruber

Cerastium tomentosum

Chamaemelum nobile

Chlorophytum comosum

Clivia miniata

Convolvulus sabatius

Coreopsis auriculata 'Nana'

Cyclamen persicum

Cymbalaria muralis

Dianthus deltoides

Dichondra micrantha

Drosanthemum floribundum

Duchesnea indica

Erigeron karvinskianus

Erodium chamaedryoides

Erysimum kotschyanum

Felicia amelloides

Festuca ovina var. glauca

Francoa ramosa

Fuchsia procumbens

Galium odoratum

Gazania 'Copper King'

Gazania rigens var. leucolaena

Geranium incanum

Glechoma hederacea

Gypsophila paniculata 'Pink Fairy'

Hedyotis caerulea

Helianthemum nummularium 'Rose'

Herniaria glabra

Heterocentron elegans

Heuchera sanguinea

Hosta sieboldiana

Hypericum coris

Iberis sempervirens

Lampranthus spectabilis

Laurentia fluviatilis

Liriope muscari

Lotus berthelotii

Lysimachia nummularia

Mentha requienii

Muehlenbeckia axillaris

Myoporum parvifolium

Nierembergia hippomanica var. violacea

Ophiopogon japonicus

Osteospermum fruticosum

Pachysandra terminalis

Pennisetum setaceum

Phlox subulata
Phyla nodiflora
Polygonum capitatum
Potentilla tabernaemontanii
Pratia angulata
Sagina subulata 'Aurea'
Saxifraga stolonifera
Sedum acre
Sedum brevifolium
Sedum confusum
Sedum rubrotinctum

Soleirolia soleirolii
Stachys byzantina
Thymus praecox arcticus
Thymus pseudolanuginosus
Tradescantia albiflora
Verbena peruviana
Veronica repens
Vinca major
Vinca minor
Viola hederacea
Viola odorata

Key to
Herbaceous Ground Cover Plants

A - Leaves bluish-gray, grayish or whitish
  B - Leaves aromatic
      Leaves pinnately lobed
         Flowers white   *Achillea ageratifolia, p. 30*
         Flowers yellow   *Achillea tomentosa, p. 32*
      Leaves not pinnately lobed
         Flowers pink   *Thymus pseudolanuginosus, p. 258*

  BB - Leaves not aromatic
    C - Leaves pinnately lobed
       Flowers yellow. Plant spreading by stolons
                   Arctotheca calendula, p. 44
       Not as above   *Gazania 'Copper King', p. 138*
    CC - Leaves not pinnately lobed
      D - Leaves grasslike
        Inflorescence a globose head. Flowers pink or whitish
                   Armeria maritima, p. 48
        Not as above   *Festuca ovina var. glauca, p. 126*
    DD - Leaves not grasslike
      E - Leaves succulent
        Leaves from 3 to 5 inches long, 1/2 inch wide
                   Carpobrotus edulis, p. 66
        Leaves 2 to 3 inches long, to 1/4 inch wide
                Lampranthus spectabilis, p. 178
        Leaves to 3/4 inch long
          Leaves with conspicuous, glistening papillae
             Drosanthemum floribundum, p. 110
         Leaves not as above   *Sedum brevifolium, p. 242*
    EE - Leaves not succulent
      F - Leaves basal
        Flowers irregular, white   *Saxifraga stolonifera, p. 238*
        Flowers regular, yellow   *Aurinia saxatilis, p. 54*
        Flowers regular, pale lavender *Hosta sieboldiana, p. 168*

      FF - Leaves alternate
        Leaves toothed
          Flowers white and fragrant   *Arabis caucasica, p. 42*
          Flowers pink to red, to purplish
                    Aubrieta deltoidea, p. 52

Leaves entire
Leaves pinnately compound, flowers scarlet
Lotus berthelotii p. 192
Leaves not compound
Flowers blue. In clusters
Convolvulus sabatius, p. 86
Flowers yellow. Solitary
Gazania rigens var. leucolaena, p. 140

FFF - Leaves opposite
Leaves toothed
Leaves 4 to 6 inches long, one inch wide.
White hairy   *Stachys byzantina, p. 254*
Leaves not as above *Phyla nodiflora, p. 218*
Leaves entire
Leaves bluish-gray. 2 to 4 inches long, to one
inch wide   *Centranthus ruber, p. 68*
Leaves not as above
Flowers yellow   *Hypericum coris, p. 172*
Flowers not yellow
Leaves white-hairy both sides
Cerastium tomentosum, p. 70
Leaves not as above
Leaves grayish-hairy
Helianthemum nummularium 'Rose', p. 160
Leaves not as above
Flowers solitary, fragrant
Dianthus deltoides, p. 106
Flowers not as above
Gypsophila paniculata 'Pink Fairy', p. 150

AA - Leaves not bluish-gray, grayish or whitish
B - Leaves compound
Leaves with 3 leaflets. Flowers yellow
Duchesnea indica, p. 112
Leaves with 5 leaflets. Flowers yellow
Potentilla tabernaemontanii, p. 222
BB - Leaves not compound
C - Leaves palmately lobed
Leaves 3 to 7-lobed. Flowers irregular, blue, solitary
Cymbalaria muralis, p. 102
Leaves 5 to 9-lobed. Flowers regular, red or pink.
In panicles   *Heuchera sanguinea, p. 166*
Leaves finely dissected. Flowers regular, purple to pink.
Solitary   *Geranium incanum, p. 142*

20

CC - **Leaves not palmately lobed**
 D - **Leaves pinnately lobed**
   Leaves aromatic   *Chamaemelum nobile, p. 74*
   Leaves not aromatic
     Leaves to 2 feet long, one foot wide. Flowers irregular,
       in spikes which are to one foot long
                                           Acanthus mollis, p. 28
       Leaves not as above
         Leaves from 6 to 12 inches long, 2 to 3 inches wide.
         Flowers in 4 to 8-inch, terminal panicles
                                           Francoa ramosa, p. 128
       Leaves not as above
         Leaves with one or 2 basal lobes. Flowers regular,
           yellow   *Coreopsis auriculata 'Nana', p. 90*
         Leaves not as above.
           Flowers regular, white
                                     Erigeron karvinskianus, p. 116
           Flowers irregular, pale blue to purple
                                       Laurentia fluviatilis, p. 182

DD - **Leaves not pinnately lobed**
  E - **Leaves succulent**
     Leaves terete or nearly so
       Flowers white   *Sedum brevifolium, p. 242*
       Flowers yellow. Leaves to 3/16 inch long, 1/8 inch wide
                                           Sedum acre, p. 240
       Flowers reddish-yellow. Leaves to 3/4 inch long,
         1/4 inch wide   *Sedum rubrotinctum, p. 246*
     Leaves not terete
       Leaves to 3/4 inch long. Flowers yellow
                                           Sedum confusum, p. 244
       Leaves 3 to 5 inches long. Flowers yellow, pink
         or purple   *Carpobrotus edulis, p. 66*
  EE - **Leaves not succulent**
     Leaves aromatic
       Leaves whorled. Flowers white, regular
                                           Galium odoratum, p. 132
       Leaves and flowers not as above. Flowers irregular
         Leaves 1/8 inch across and as long. Flowers a
           light purple   *Mentha requienii, p. 196*
         Leaves 1/4 inch across and as long. Flowers
           purplish-white   *Thymus praecox arcticus, p. 256*

     Leaves not aromatic
     Leaves grasslike

21

Leaves to 4 inches long. Flowers pink to whitish,
  in a head   *Armeria maritima, p. 48*
Leaves to 12 inches long. Flowers light purple
              Ophiopogon japonicus, p. 204
Leaves to 3 feet long. Inflorescence not as above
              Pennisetum setaceum, p. 212

Leaves not grasslike
  Leaves straplike
    Leaves 2-ranked. Flowers scarlet
              Clivia miniata, p. 82
    Leaves not as above
      Leaves to 2 inches wide. Flowers blue
              Agapanthus orientalis, p. 32
      Leaves to 1/2 inch wide. Flowers blue
        Agapanthus orientalis 'Peter Pan', p. 34
      Leaves to 3/4 inch wide. Flowers a dark purple
              Liriope, muscari, p. 186
  Leaves not straplike
F - Leaves opposite
 G - Leaves toothed
    Flowers reddish
      Flowers purplish-red. Regular
              Heterocentron elegans, p. 164
      Flowers red (cultivars are also other
      colors). Irregular   *Verbena peruviana, p. 264*
    Flowers blue to violet
      Leaves to 4 inches long, 2 to 3 inches
      wide   *Ajuga reptans, p. 38*
    Not as above
      Flowers in dense heads
              Phyla nodiflora, p. 218
      Flowers in axillary verticillasters
              Glechoma hederacea, p. 144
      Flowers solitary or in few-flowered
      racemes   *Veronica repens, p. 266*
 GG - Leaves entire
    Flowers yellow   *Lysimachia nummularia, p. 194*
    Flowers white
      Crowded in axillary clusters *Herniaria glabra, p.162*
      Mostly solitary and terminal
              Sagina subulata 'Aurea', p. 232
    Flowers blue to lavender or white. Solitary
      1/2 inch across   *Hedyotis caerulea, p. 158*
    Flowers pink, red or purplish. Each
      to 3/4 inch across. In terminal panicles
               Phlox subulata, p. 216

Flowers pink, solitary   *Dianthus deltoides, p. 106*
Flowers blue, with yellow stamens. In heads
    to 1 1/4 inches across   *Felicia amelloides, p. 124*
Flowers and inflorescence not as above
    Leaves 2 to 3 inches long, to one inch wide
      Flowers one to 2 inches across   *Vinca major, p. 270*

    Leaves 1 1/2 to 2 inches long, to 3/4 inch
      wide. Flowers to one inch across   *Vinca minor, p. 272*

FF - Leaves alternate
  G - Leaves toothed
    Flowers regular
      Flowers bright yellow   *Erysimum kotschyanum, p. 120*
      Flowers red to orange   *Fuchsia procumbens, p. 130*
      Flowers purple to lavender
        Leaves to one inch long and about as wide.
         Flowers campanulate
           Campanula portenschlagiana, p. 62

        Leaves 1 to 3 1/2 inches long and about as wide.
         Flowers stellate   *Campanula poscharskyana, p. 64*
      Flowers white
        Leaves warty both sides   *Myoporum parvifolium, p. 200*
        Leaves not as above
         Flowers in heads. To 2 inches across
           Osteospermum fruticosum, p. 206
         Flowers in 3 to 4 inch spikes
           Pachysandra terminalis, p. 208
         Flowers solitary and axillary   *Pratia angulata, p. 224*
    Flowers irregular
      Flowers violet. Very fragrant. Leaves bumpy on upper side
          . *Viola odorata, p. 276*
      Flowers and leaves not as above   *Viola hederacea, p. 274*

  GG - Leaves entire
    Leaves 2 to 3 inches long, to one inch wide.
      Flowers with 3 petals.   *Tradescantia albiflora, p. 262*
    Leaves to 1 1/2 inches long, to one inch wide.
      With reddish-brown markings. Stems reddish,
      jointed   *Polygonum capitatum, p. 220*

    Leaves to 1 1/2 inches long, to 1/4 inch wide
      White glaucous below   *Andromeda polifolia 'Nana', p. 40*
      Not as above   *Iberis sempervirens, p. 174*

Leaves to one inch long. 1/8 inch or more wide
Flowers blue to violet. Solitary and terminal
*Nierembergia hippomanica
var. violacea*,   *p. 202*

Leaves 1/2 to one inch long. To 1/4 inch wide.
Warty both sides. Flowers white. Solitary or
in axillary clusters
Myoporum parvifolium, p. 200

Leaves 1/2 to one inch long and as wide. Orbicular,
or cordate to reniform. Flowers greenish-
yellow   *Dichondra micrantha , p. 108*

Leaves to 1/4 inch long and as wide. Oblong
to nearly orbicular. Stems wiry. Flowers
very small. Yellowish-green. Solitary or
in twos's   *Muehlenbeckia axillaris, p. 198*

Leaves to 1/4 inch long and as wide. Flowers
white to greenish. Solitary and axillary
Soleirolia soleirolii, p. 250

FFF - **Leaves basal**
 G - **Leaves entire**
   Leaves grasslike
     Leaves 12-18 inches long, to 3/4 inch wide
Chlorophytum comosum, p. 76

   Leaves not grasslike
     Leaves very large   *Hosta sieboldiana, p. 168*

GG - **Leaves toothed**
   Flowers regular
     Leaves to 8 inches long, 4 to 6 inches wide
Bergenia crassifolia, p. 58

     Leaves to 3 inches long and as wide. Plant
       10 to 12 inches high   *Cyclamen persicum, p. 100*
     Leaves to 1/2 inch long and as wide.
       Plant 3 to 6 inches high
Erodium chamaedryoides p. 118

   Flowers irregular
     Flowers violet. Very fragrant. Leaves
       bumpy on upper side   *Viola odorata, p. 276*
     Flowers and leaves not as above
       Leaves 2 to 4 inches across. Veins
         grayish above   *Saxifraga stolonifera, p. 238*

     Leaves not as above   *Viola hederacea, p. 274*

DESCRIPTIONS
of
GROUND COVER PLANTS

Acanthus mollis

Family Acanthaceae

Leaves Evergreen. An herbaceous perennial. Opposite. Mostly basal. Pinnately lobed. Lobes toothed. Oblong to ovate. Somewhat cordate. Veins conspicuous. Hairy on lower side. Glabrous, dark glossy green above. Glandular-dotted both sides. 2 to 3 feet long and about half as wide. Stems sparsely pubescent, glandular-dotted and somewhat angular.

Flowers Whitish, rose or lilac. In spikes which are to 1 1/2 feet long on 2 foot stalks. With greenish or purplish bracts. Irregular. Corolla with a single, expanded, 3-lobed lip. Stamens 4. Late spring or early summer into the fall.

Fruit About 1 1/4 inches long. A 2-celled capsule, with 2 seeds to the capsule.

Environment Best in some shade. Tolerant to considerable shade and to below zero.

Pests Caterpillars. Slugs. Snails.

Propagation Seed. Division.

Rate of Growth Moderate to rapid

Pruning Can be cut to the ground after bloom. Remove unattractive leaves as needed. Keep under control. Spreads by rhizomes.

Seasonal Value Foliage. Flowers.

Shape Upright. Arching.

Spread 6 feet or more

Height 2 to 3 feet

Soil Best in a rich, moist soil, but fairly tolerant. For best appearance, needs sufficient moisture.

Use Ground cover. Borders. Containers. Dry arrangements. Tropical effect.

Origin Africa. Asia. Europe.

Comments *Acanthus* means thorn. Some species are spinose. The leaf of Acanthus is seen in ancient art, as on Corinthian and Egyptian columns. Other species include *baleanicus, latifolius, lusitanicus* and *montanus.*

Achillea ageratifolia

BEAR'S BREECH

Family Compositae

Leaves Evergreen. An herbaceous perennial. Alternate, fascicled or in basal rosettes. Entire, crenate, dentate or pinnately lobed. Oblanceolate to spatulate. Pubescent and silvery-gray both sides. Aromatic. To 1 1/2 inches long. 1/8 to 1/4 inch wide. Stems brownish.

Flowers A brilliant white. In solitary heads. To one inch across. Ray flowers white. Regular. Corolla 4 to 5-lobed. Stamens 4 to 5. Stems 4 to 10 inches long. Summer to early fall.

Fruit An achene, with no pappus.

Environment Full sun best. Tolerant to below zero.

Pests Aphids. Caterpillars, Soil Mealybug. Slugs. Snails.

Propagation Seed. Divison.

Rate of Growth Moderate

Pruning Remove dead flowers.

Seasonal Value Foliage. Flowers.

Shape Mat-forming

Spread To one foot or more

Height To 8 inches or more

Soil Best when light, sandy, well-drained. Tolerant to drought once established.

Use Ground cover. Rock gardens.

Origin Greece

Comments Was once *Anthemis ageratifolia*. Achillea species are said to have been used by Achilles because of their healing properties. The variety *aizoon* has leaves that are mostly entire. These plants are said to be fire-resistant.

Achillea tomentosa

Family   Compositae

Leaves   Evergreen. An herbaceous perennial. Alternate or in basal rosettes. Twice-pinnately dissected. Segments entire and each linear to lanceolate. Tomentose both sides. Grayish. Aromatic. To 2 inches long. Each segment to 1/4 inch long. Stems angular and hairy.

Flowers   Yellow. In heads about 3/16 inch across. In dense corymbs. Disc and ray flowers yellow. Regular. Corolla 4 to 5-lobed. Stamens 4 or 5. May to September.

Fruit   An achene with no pappus.

Environment   Full sun best. To below zero.

Pests   Aphids. Caterpillars. Soil Mealybug. Slugs. Snails.

Propagation   Seed. Divison.

Rate of Growth   Rapid

Pruning   Remove dead flowers. Keep under control. Spreads by short stolons.

Seasonal Value   Foliage. Flowers. Fragrance (Leaves).

Shape   Mat-forming

Spread   Wide

Height   6 to 12 inches

Soil   Tolerant to soils and to drought when established. Best in a dry situation.

Use   Ground cover. Edging. Rock gardens. Dry arrangements. Between stepping stones.

Origin   Asia. Europe.

Comments   Cultivars include 'Aurea', 'King George', 'Moonlight', 'Nana' and 'Primrose Beauty.'

Agapanthus orientalis

Family   Amaryllidaceae

Leaves   Evergreen. An herbaceous perennial. Basal. Entire. Broadly linear. Straplike. Glabrous and with white dots on both sides. Parallel-veined, with a conspicuous midrib. Dark green and glossy above. Leaves about 10 to a clump. 2 feet or more in length. To 2 inches wide.

Flowers   Blue. Funnelform. 2 to 3 inches across. In 40 to 110-flowered unbels. Regular. Perianth 6-lobed. Stamens 6. Summer and into the fall.

Fruit   A capsule

Environment   Full sun in cool areas. Usually best in some shade. Tolerant to considerable shade. Better leaf color in shade. 20 to 25 degrees.

Pests   Root Knot Nematode. Soil Mealybug. Said to be resistant to deer, but is not.

Propagation   Seed. Division.

Rate of Growth   Moderate to rapid

Pruning   Remove dead flowers, leaves. Divide periodically. Spreads by rhizomes.

Seasonal Value   Foliage. Flowers.

Shape   Mound-forming

Spread   Several feet or more.

Height   2 feet or more.

Soil   Tolerant, but best if fertile and with sufficient water. Drought-tolerant when established. Needs water when flowering.

Use   Ground cover. Containers. Cut flowers. Indoors.

Origin   South Africa

Comments   Has a number of cultivars, including 'Peter Pan'. *Agapanthus* means Love-Flower. This plant has been named *A. umbellatus* and *A. africanus*. However, the latter has leaves that are to 20 inches long and to 1/2 inch wide. Also, the flowers of the latter are in 12 to 30-flowered umbels.

Agapanthus orientalis
'Peter Pan'

DWARF LILY-OF-THE-NILE

Family Amaryllidaceae

Leaves Evergreen. An herbaceous perennial. Entire. Basal. Linear. Straplike. Glabrous, and with white dots on both sides, especially on the lower. Parallel-veined, with a conspicuous midrib. Dark green and glossy above. About 12 inches or more in length. About 1/2 inch wide.

Flowers Blue. Funnelform. In terminal umbels. On stems which are about one foot or more long. Regular. Perianth 6-lobed. Stamens 6. Summer-fall.

Fruit A capsule which is about 3/4 inch long.

Environment Full sun or partial shade. Usually best in some, and tolerant to considerable shade. 10 to 15 degrees.

Pests Root Knot Nematode. Soil Mealybug. Slugs. Snails.

Propagation Division

Rate of Growth Rapid

Pruning Remove dead flowers, leaves. Divide periodically. Produces thick rhizomes.

Seasonal Value Foliage. Flowers.

Shape Clumping

Spread 1 to 2 feet

Height 8 to 12 inches

Soil Best when fertile, moist, but tolerant to soils and to drought. Provide good drainage.

Use Ground cover. Borders. Containers. Cut flowers.

Origin The parent plant is from South Africa.

Comments More appropriate in smaller landscapes than the parent plant.

Ajuga Reptans

Family Labiatae

Leaves Evergreen or nearly so. An herbaceous perennial.Basal or opposite. Crenate or nearly entire. Spatulate, ovate, or obovate. Mature leaves glabrous and glandular-dotted both sides. Dark green. Bronzy in cold weather. Thin. To 4 inches long. 2 to 3 inches wide. Stems squarish, mostly glabrous and often reddish.

Flowers Blue to purple. Campanulate. In upright, terminal spikes (verticillasters). To 4 inches high. Irregular. Corolla usually 5-lobed. Stamens 4. From fall or winter until the following summer.

Fruit Consisting of 4 obovoid nutlets.

Environment Usually best in partial shade. Tolerant to full sun in cooler areas. Tolerant to considerable shade. To below zero.

Pests Aphids. Mites. Nematodes. Slugs. Snails. Crown Rot. Mildew.

Propagation Seed. Cuttings. Division.

Rate of Growth Rapid

Pruning Remove dead flowers. Keep under control. Invasive. Spreads by stolons.

Seasonal Value Foliage. Flowers. Winter color (Foliage and flowers).

Shape Mat-forming. Trailing.

Spread Wide

Height To 12 inches

Soil Best when fertile, organic, well-drained. Needs sufficient water. Responds to periodic fertilizing.

Use Ground cover. Rock gardens. Slopes. Between stepping stones. Over walls.

Origin Europe

Comments *reptans* means creeping. The plant is not tolerant to foot traffic. Cultivars include 'Giant Bronze', 'Jungle Bronze', 'Jungle Green', 'Purpurea', 'Variegata'.

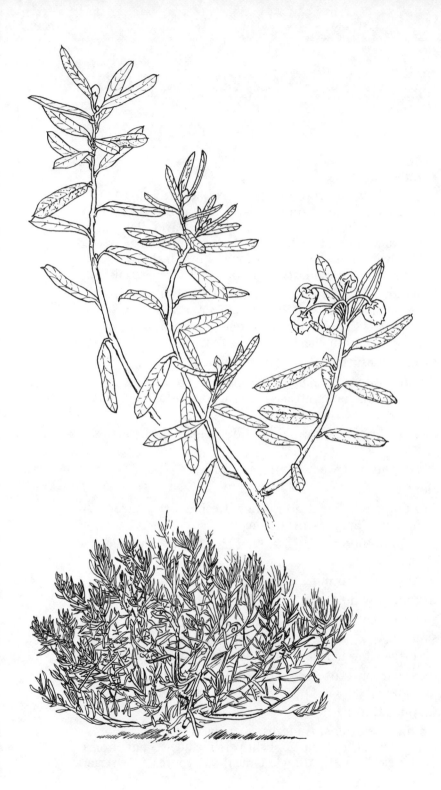

Andromeda polifolia 'Nana'

BOG ROSEMARY

Family Ericaceae

Leaves Evergreen. Alternate. Entire. Linear to oblong. Cuspidate. Revolute. Coriaceous. Conspicuously net-veined. Midrib conspicuous below and depressed above. Glabrous both sides. Dark green above, white glaucous below. To 1 1/2 inches long. About 1/4 inch wide.

Flowers Pink, fading to white. Urn-shaped. To 1/4 inch across. In terminal, pendulous umbels. Mostly regular. Corolla 5-lobed. Stamens 10. April-May.

Fruit A 5-valved capsule

Environment Full sun or partial shade. To below zero.

Pests Aphids. Thrips. Mites.

Propagation Seed. Cuttings. Layering.

Rate of Growth Moderate

Pruning Keep under control. Spreads by rhizomes.

Seasonal Value Foliage. Flowers.

Shape Compact. Stiff. Upright.

Spread Wide

Height To 12 inches

Soil Acid, with sufficient moisture. Tolerant to wet situations.

Use Ground cover. Bog gardens. Rock gardens.

Origin Asia. Europe. North America.

Comments *polifolia* means white. The leaves resemble those of Rosemary, hence the common name. Cultivars include 'Angustifolia', 'Compacta', 'Grandiflora Compacta', 'Major', 'Minima', 'Montana' and 'Nana'.

Arabis caucasica

WALL ROCKCRESS

Family   Cruciferae

Leaves   Evergreen. An herbaceous perennial. Alternate or in terminal fascicles. Dentate. Mostly with 3 teeth on each side. Spatulate to obovate. Obtuse. White pubescent and glandular-dotted both sides. Grayish. To one inch long and to 1/2 inch wide.

Flowers   White. 1/2 to one inch across. In loose racemes. Fragrant. Regular. Petals 4. Stamens 6. Flowers profuse. Spring.

Fruit   A long, narrow silique, 1 1/2 to 2 1/2 inches in length.

Environment   Full sun or partial shade. Shade where warm. Does well or better with cold winters. To below zero.

Pests   Aphids. Leaf Miner. Soil Mealybug. Leaf Spot. Mildew.

Propagation   Seed. Cuttings. Division.

Rate of Growth   Moderate

Pruning   Keep under control. Spreads by stolons.

Seasonal Value   Foliage. Flowers. Fragrance (Flowers).

Shape   Mat-forming. Tufted.

Spread   1 1/2 feet or more.

Height   6 inches or more.

Soil   Best when fertile, well-drained. Drought-tolerant, but does well with moderate watering.

Use   Ground cover. Rock gardens. Effective in small areas.

Origin   Europe to Iran

Comments   *caucasica* means from the Caucasus region. Was once *A. albida* and *A. billardieri*. The cultivars include 'Floroplena', 'Pink Charm', 'Rosabella' and 'Variegata'. The plant resembles *Aubrieta deltoidea;* however, the latter is more straggly and the flowers are from pink to red to purplish.

Arctotheca calendula

Family   Compositae

Leaves   Evergreen. An herbaceous perennial. Alternate or fascicled. Entire to dentate. Deeply and odd-pinnately lobed. Sparsely hairy above. White tomentose below. Dark green above, but appearing grayish. 6 to 8 inches long. To 2 inches wide. Stems hairy.

Flowers   Yellow. To 2 inches across. Profuse. In heads. Regular. Corolla 4 to 5-lobed. Stamens 5. Mostly in the spring, but also intermittent throughout the year.

Fruit   An achene

Environment   Full sun. To about 25 degrees.

Pests   Aphids

Propagation   Cuttings. Division.

Rate of Growth   Rapid

Pruning   Keep under control. Very invasive. Spreads by stolons. Seed apparently not viable, at least in San Francisco Bay Area.

Seasonal Value   Foliage. Flowers.

Shape   Prostrate. Sprawling

Spread   Wide

Height   8 to 12 inches

Soil   Tolerant to soils and to drought, but best with some water.

Use   Ground cover. Containers. Erosion control. Hanging baskets. Slopes. Over walls.

Origin   Africa

Comments   The word *calendula* means resembling the Pot Marigold, the genus of which is *Calendula*.

Ardisia japonica

Family Myrsinaceae

Leaves Evergreen. Alternate. In terminal whorls. Elliptic. Serrate. Glabrous and glandular-dotted both sides. Bright green. Coriaceous. To 4 inches long. To one inch wide. Stems reddish to brown.

Flowers White. Each to 1/4 inch across. 2 to 6 in a cluster. Regular. Corolla 5-parted. Stamens 5. Fall.

Fruit A bright red, glabrous drupe. To 1/4 inch across. Winter.

Environment Best in partial shade. To 25 or 30 degrees.

Pests Aphids. Hemispherical Scale. Leaf Spot. Root Knot Nematode.

Propagation Seed. Cuttings.

Rate of Growth Moderate

Pruning Keep under control. Spreads by rhizomes.

Seasonal Value Foliage. Flowers. Fall and winter color (Flowers, fruit).

Shape Erect

Spread 2 to 3 feet

Height 6 to 18 inches

Soil Best with sufficient water

Use Ground cover. Containers. Shade areas.

Origin China. Japan.

Comments *Ardisia* means point, referring to the stamens or to the corolla lobes.

Armeria maritima

Family Plumbaginaceae

Leaves Evergreen. An herbaceous perennial. Basal. Entire. Narrowly linear to lanceolate. Grasslike. One-nerved. Glabrous and glandular-dotted both sides. Grayish or green. To 4 inches long. 1/8 inch wide or less.

Flowers Pink or whitish. There are many flowers in a globose head which is to one inch across. The head is terminal and solitary at the end of a naked scape which may be 12 inches or more in length. Regular. Petals 5. Stamens 5. All summer and intermittently throughout the year.

Fruit A membranous utricle. 5-pointed at the apex.

Environment Full sun. Tolerant to partial shade and to seacoast conditions. To below zero.

Pests Soil Mealybug. Slugs. Snails.

Propagation Seed. Division

Rate of Growth Moderate

Pruning Remove dead flowers.

Seasonal Value Foliage. Flowers.

Shape A tuft or mound.

Spread To 12 inches

Height 6 to 8 inches

Soil Best if fertile, well-drained and with sufficient water.

Use Ground cover. Borders. Containers. Rock gardens. Slopes. Effective grouped in small areas.

Origin Asia Minor. Chile. North Africa. North America.

Comments Former names include *Statice armeria, S. maritima, S. maritima var. laucheana, Armeria vulgaris* and *A. vulgaris var. pubescens.* Cultivars include 'Laucheana' and 'Six Hills'.

49

Asparagus densiflorus 'Sprengeri'

Family Liliaceae

Leaves Evergreen. Somewhat woody. Alternate, whorled or fascicled. Entire. Linear. Somewhat needlelike. Glabrous and glandular-dotted both sides. Slightly curved. A glossy, yellowish-green. Cuspidate. One-nerved. To one inch long. 1/8 inch wide. Stems 3 feet or more in length, stiff, parallel-ridged, glandular-dotted and spinose.

Flowers White or pale pink. About 1/2 inch across. In axillary racemes. Fragrant. Perianth of 6 segments. Stamens 6. Regular. Summer-fall.

Fruit Berries, each of which is about 1/4 inch across and turning from green to bright red. Winter period.

Environment Full sun in cool areas, but usually best in partial shade. Here the foliage is a darker color. To 35 or 40 degrees.

Pests Aphids. Caterpillars. Scales. Thrips. Mites. Crown Gall. Root Rot.

Propagation Division

Rate of Growth Moderate

Pruning Keep under control. Spreads by rhizomes and by tuberous roots.

Seasonal Value Foliage. Flowers. Fragrance (Flowers). Fruit. Winter color (Fruit).

Shape Arching, Twining

Spread To about 6 feet

Height 3 feet on ground. To 6 feet with support.

Soil Best if fertile, with sufficient moisture.

Use Ground cover. Hanging baskets. Indoor planters. Vine.

Origin South Africa

Comments Formerly was *A. sprengeri.* Is the most commonly used of Asparagus species. Garden Asparagus is *A. officinalis.* What appear to be leaves are actually cladodes. These perform all of the functions of leaves. Cultivars include 'Meyers', 'Sprengeri Deflexus', 'Sprengeri Nanus', 'Sprengeri Robustus' and 'Sprengeri Compacta'.

Aubrieta deltoidea

Family Cruciferae

Leaves Evergreen. An herbaceous perennial. Alternate. With one or more teeth on either side. Spatulate to rhomboidal. Hairy on both sides, with stellate or forked hairs. Glandular-dotted both sides. Grayish. To 1 1/4 inches long and about 1/2 inch wide. Stems hairy.

Flowers Pink to red or purplish. To 3/4 inch across. In short, terminal racemes. Regular. Petals 4. Stamens 6. Early spring.

Fruit A broadly elliptic silique. To 3/4 inch long.

Environment Full sun. Partial shade where hot. To below zero.

Pests Aphids. Soil Mealybug.

Propagation Seed. Cuttings. Division.

Rate of Growth Moderate

Pruning Cut back after flowering.

Seasonal Value Foliage. Flowers.

Shape Mat-forming, mounding.

Spread 1 to 1 1/2 feet

Height 6 to 12 inches

Soil Tolerant to soils and to drought. Needs some water for flowering. Provide good drainage.

Use Ground cover. Between stepping stones. Rock gardens. In and on walls.

Origin Greece. Sicily to Asia Minor.

Comments Was once *Alyssum deltoideum*. Related to and resembling Arabis. The latter has more teeth and the flowers are white.

Aurinia saxatilis

BASKET-OF-GOLD

Family Cruciferae

Leaves Evergreen. An herbaceous perennial. Basal. In tufted rosettes. Entire. Repand. Oblanceolate to spatulate. White tomentose both sides. Grayish. 2 to 5 inches long. About 1/2 inch wide.

Flowers Golden yellow. About 1/4 inch across. In panicles. Regular. Petals 4. Stamens 6. Spring and early summer.

Fruit A suborbicular, glabrous silicle.

Environment Full sun or partial shade. Does well in sun. To below zero.

Pests Aphids. Soil Mealybug.

Propagation Seed. Cuttings. Self-sows.

Rate of Growth Moderate

Pruning Cut back lightly after flowering.

Seasonal Value Foliage. Flowers.

Shape Mat-forming, mounding.

Spread 12 inches or more   To 12 inches

Soil Best with some water. Must be well-drained. Tolerant to drought, poor soil.

Use Ground cover. Borders. Rock gardens. Over walls.

Origin Europe. Turkey.

Comments Formerly *Alyssum arduini, A. orientale* and *A. saxatile*. Cultivars include 'Citrina', 'Compacta', 'Lutea', 'Nana', 'Plena', 'Silver Queen' and 'Sulphurea'.

Berberis
stenophylla 'Irwinii'

Family Berberidaceae

Leaves Evergreen. Alternate or whorled. Mostly entire, except for the apex which is 3-lobed. Each lobe is cuspidate. Oblanceolate. Revolute. Glabrous and glandular-dotted both sides. Dark green above and grayish below. Some coloring of the leaves during cold weather. To one inch long. 1/4 inch wide. Stems with 3-parted spines and somewhat hairy.

Folowers Yellow. In pendulous racemes. Each flower about 1/2 inch across. 7 to 14 in a raceme. Regular. Petals 6. Stamens 6. Spring.

Fruit A globose, black or purplish berry. Glaucous. About 1/2 inch across. Spring-summer.

Environment Full sun or partial shade. To below zero.

Pests Aphids. Mealybug.

Propagation Cuttings

Rate of Growth Moderate

Pruning Remove any dead wood.

Seasonal Value Foliage. Flowers, Fruit. Fall color (Leaves).

Shape Stiff. Upright.

Spread 1 1/2 to 2 feet

Height 18 inches

Soil Tolerant to soils and to some drought. Best, however, with some water.

Use Ground cover. Barrier. Rock gardens.

Origin A cultivar, as is the parent plant.

Comments *stenophylla* means narrow-leaved. The wood and bark of this and other Berberis species are of a yellow color and are often used in dyeing.

Bergenia crassifolia

WINTER-BLOOMING BERGENIA

Family Saxifragaceae

Leaves Evergreen. An herbaceous perennial. Basal. Usually crenate or serrate. Elliptic to oblong or obovate. Usually not cordate at the base. Glabrous and glandular-dotted both sides. Coriaceous. Medium green. To 8 inches long. From 4 to 6 inches wide. Stems glabrous.

Flowers Pink to purplish. Each to 3/4 inch across. In upright and somewhat pendulous panicles. Regular. Petals 5. Stamens 10. Mostly from January into summer, but also intermittently throughout the year.

Fruit A capsule

Environment Partial shade best. Tolerant to full sun in cool areas. To 15 degrees.

Pests Aphids. Mealybug. Thrips. Weevils. Slugs. Snails.

Propagation Seed. Division.

Rate of Growth Slow to moderate.

Pruning Remove dead flowers. Thin periodically. Keep under control. Invasive. Has thick rhizomes.

Seasonal Value Foliage. Flowers. Winter color (Flowers).

Shape Mounding

Spread Wide

Height 12 to 18 inches

Soil Tolerant to soils and to drought, but best with sufficient water. Best if slightly alkaline.

Use Ground cover. Borders. Planters. Raised beds.

Origin Mongolia and Siberia. Found at elevations of from 8000 to 14,000 feet.

Comments Was once *Saxifraga crassifolia* and *Bergenia bifolia*. The plant becomes rampant and unattractive with neglect.

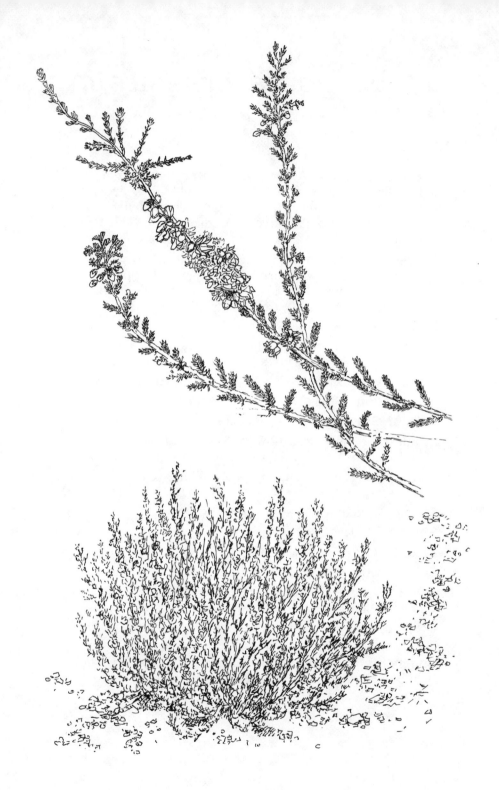

Calluna vulgaris

Family Ericaceae

Leaves Evergreen. Opposite. 4-ranked. Entire, or apparently so. Imbricated. Scalelike or awl-shaped. Glabrous or pubescent. Dark green. Turning bronzy in the fall or winter. About 1/10 inch long. About 1/16 inch wide. Stems angular, reddish and hairy.

Flowers Rosy or purplish-pink. Each about 1/8 inch across. Campanulate. Usually regular. Corolla 4 to 5-lobed. Stamens 8. In terminal, one-sided, spikelike racemes which are to 10 inches in length. Summer and fall.

Fruit A capsule

Environment Full sun. Partial shade where hot. To below zero.

Pests Aphids. Scale insects.

Propagation Seed. Cuttings. Division.

Rate of Growth Moderate to rapid.

Pruning Remove dead flowers and then head back lightly.

Seasonal Value Foliage. Flowers.

Shape Upright. Rounded.

Spread 2 to 3 feet

Height 2 to 3 feet

Soil Tolerant to poor soils if well-drained. Best when acid, fertile and moist. Responds to periodic fertilizing.

Use Ground cover. Rock gardens.

Origin Asia Minor. Europe.

Comments Formerly *Erica vulgaris*. *Calluna* means to sweep. Apparently the branches were once used for brooms. *vulgaris* means common. There are many cultivars, and by using the various ones, color can be had from summer to fall. The size of the plant may vary also, from several inches to several feet.

Campanula portenschlagiana

DALMATIAN BELLFLOWER

Family Campanulaceae

Leaves Evergreen. An herbaceous perennial. Alternate. Crenate to serrate. Orbicular to cordate. Nearly lobed at the base. Glabrous and glandular-dotted both sides. Medium to dark green. Basal leaves often larger than those on the stem. From one to 1 1/2 inches wide and about as long. Stems somewhat angular.

Flowers Purple. To one inch long, to 3/4 inch across. 2 to 3 flowers on each stem. Usually in racemes. Campanulate. Regular. Corolla 5-lobed but not lobed beyond the middle. Stamens 5. May-August, or longer.

Fruit A capsule. To 3/4 inch long.

Environment Full sun in cooler areas. Partial shade where warm. To below zero.

Pests Aphids. Soil Mealybug. Thrips. Mites. Slugs. Snails. Crown Rot. Leaf Spot. Mildew.

Propagation Seed. Cuttings. Division.

Rate of Growth Moderate to rapid.

Pruning Remove dead flowers. Cut back severely. Divide periodically. Spreads by slender rhizomes.

Seasonal Value Foliage. Flowers.

Shape Mat-forming

Spread Wide

Height 4 to 8 inches

Soil Best when light, fertile, well-drained.

Use Ground cover. Borders. Containers. Hanging Baskets. Rock gardens. Over walls.

Origin Yugoslavia

Comments Was once *C. muralis*. This plant is more moderate in growth habit than is *C. poscharskyana*.

Campanula poscharskyana

SERBIAN BELLFLOWER

Family   Campanulaceae

Leaves   Evergreen. An herbaceous perennial. Alternate. Irregularly toothed. Nearly crenate, or serrate. Cordate to ovate or orbicular. Acute. Glabrous and glandular-dotted both sides. Ciliate. Medium green. Base somewhat auricled. One to 3 1/2 inches long and about as wide. Stems somewhat angular.

Flowers   Lavender. Stellate. Each to 1 1/4 inch across. Funnelform. Regular. Corolla deeply 5-lobed. Stamens 5. Spring to early summer.

Fruit   A capsule

Environment   Full sun where cooler. Partial shade elsewhere. To below zero.

Pests   Aphids. Soil Mealybug. Thrips. Slugs. Snails. Crown Rot. Leaf Spot. Mildrew.

Propagation   Seed. Cuttings. Division.

Rate of Growth   Moderate to rapid

Pruning   Remove dead flowers. Keep under control. Spreads by slender rhizomes. A vigorous grower.

Seasonal Value   Foliage. Flowers.

Shape   Mat-forming

Spread   Wide

Height   12 inches or more.

Soil   Best in an acid, fertile, moist soil. Provide good drainage.

Use   Ground cover. Borders. Containers. Rock gardens.

Origin   Yugoslavia

Comments   *Campanula* means little bell. This is a more vigorous grower than is *C. portenschlagiana*.

Carpobrotus edulis

HOTTENTOT FIG

Family Aizoaceae

Leaves Evergreen. An herbaceous perennial. Opposite. Entire, except for the keel, which is minutely serrate. Linear. 3-angled. Glabrous and glandular-dotted all sides. Green to grayish. Succulent. Keel reddish, and reddish coloring on leaves when plant is under stress. 3 to 5 inches long. 1/2 inch wide. Stems glabrous and reddish.

Flowers Light yellow to rose -pink or purple. To 4 inches across. Solitary. Opening in the sun. Regular. Petals many. Stamens many. Summer.

Fruit A fleshy or pulpy and indehiscent capsule. Edible, but not especially tasty.

Environment Full sun. To about 25 degrees.

Pests Ice Plant Scale. Snails and Slugs. Leaf spots.

Propagation Seed. Cuttings. Division.

Rate of Growth Rapid

Pruning Keep under control. Will naturalize. Spreads by stolons.

Seasonal Value Foliage. Flowers.

Shape Decumbent. Sprawling.

Spread Wide

Height To 12 inches

Soil Tolerant to soils and to some drought, but best when soil is fertile and has some water.

Use Ground cover. For moderate slopes.

Origin South Africa

Comments Was formerly *Mesembryanthemum edulis*. *Carpobrotus* refers to the edible fruit. Not effective for erosion control on steep slopes because the branches are heavy and the plant will move when the soil moves. Fire-resistant. Differs from *C. chilensis* in that the latter has straight sides which are only 2 inches long. Also, the latter has a keel which is not serrate and flowers which are rosy-purple. The leaves of *C. edulis* are somewhat curved.

Centranthus ruber

Family Valerianaceae

Leaves Evergreen. An herbaceous perennial or partly woody. Opposite. Entire. Ovate to lanceolate. Midrib conspicuous. Glabrous, glaucous and glandular-dotted both sides. Bluish-gray. From 2 to 4 inches long. 1/2 to one inch wide. Stems glabrous and glandular-dotted.

Flowers Pink to red. Each about 1/3 inch across and 1/2 inch long. Tubular. In dense, terminal clusters. Fragrant. Regular. Corolla 5-lobed. Stamens one. Spring-summer and longer.

Fruit A one-seeded, one-celled nut. With a pappus.

Environment Full sun to partial shade. Very tolerant to adverse conditions. To 15 degrees.

Pests Aphids. Mealybug.

Propagation Seed. Division. Self-sows.

Rate of Growth Rapid

Pruning Prune to shape and to stimulate flowering, and also to keep under control. Invasive.

Seasonal Value Foliage. Flowers. Fragrance (Flowers).

Shape Upright. Sprawling.

Spread Wide

Height To 3 feet

Soil Tolerant to soils, to drought and to alkalinity.

Use Ground cover. Cut flowers. Informal borders. Slopes. Specimen.

Origin Europe and the Mediterranean area.

Comments Formerly *Kentranthus ruber, Valeriana ruber* and *V. coccinea. Centranthus* means spurred flower *ruber* means red. This plant has naturalized in many areas of the western United States. The cultivars include 'Albus', 'Atrococcineus' and 'Roseus'.

Cerastium tomentosum

SNOW-IN-SUMMER

Family Caryophyllaceae

Leaves Evergreen. An herbaceous perennial. Opposite. Entire. Oblong or oblanceolate to lanceolate or even spatulate. Midrib conspicuous. Glandular-dotted and white tomentose both sides. 3/4 to one inch long. To 1/4 inch wide. Stems pubescent and squarish.

Flowers White. Each 1/2 to 3/4 inch across. With peduncles to 6 inches long. Borne in 3 to 15- flowered, terminal cymes. Protruding above the foliage. Regular. Petals deeply divided and usually 5. Stamens 5 to 10. Prolific. Spring-summer or longer.

Fruit A cylindrical capsule which is often curled. Dehiscing at the top into 10 parts.

Environment Full sun best. Tolerant to desert heat and to coastal fog. To below zero.

Pests Aphids. Mealybug. Soil Mealybug.

Propagation Seed. Cuttings. Division.

Rate of Growth Rapid

Pruning Can be cut back after flowering.

Seasonal Value Foliage. Flowers.

Shape Mat-forming

Spread Wide

Height 6 to 8 inches

Soil Best in a poor soil. Drought tolerant. Good drainage important. Will benefit from periodic fertilizing.

Use Ground cover. Borders. Planters. Rock gardens. Between stepping stone.

Origin Europe

Comments Formerly *C. columnae*. *Cerastium* means horn, referring to the shape of the capsule. Looks rather ragged in the winter season, but recovers with warmer weather.

70

Ceratostigma plumbaginoides

Family Plumbaginaceae

Leaves Nearly evergreen. Alternate. Entire. Oblanceolate to obovate or spatulate. Glabrous and glandular-dotted both sides. Ciliate, with somewhat reddish hairs. Medium green, but becoming bronzy or reddish with stress. To 1 1/2 inches long. Width about 3/4 to one inch. Young stems hairy. Older stems squarish and sparsely hairy. hairy.

Flowers A brilliant gentian blue. Each to 1/2 inch across. Stellate and salverform. In dense heads. Regular. Corolla 5-lobed. Stamens 5. Summer to fall.

Fruit A 5-valved capsule.

Environment Full sun to partial shade. To 10 or 20 degrees.

Pest Aphids

Propagation Seed. Cuttings. Division. Self-sows.

Rate of Growth Slow to start. Rapid once established.

Pruning Cut back each winter. Keep under control. Aggressive. Spreads by rhizomes.

Seasonal Value Foliage. Flowers. Fall color (Flowers and foliage).

Shape Prostrate. Sprawling.

Spread Wide

Height 6 to 15 inches

Soil Tolerant to soils and to those somewhat alkaline. Provide good drainage.

Use Ground cover. Erosion control. Slopes.

Origin China

Comments *Ceratostigma* means horned stigma. This plant was once *Plumbago larpentiae*. Other species include *griffithii* and *willmotianum*.

Chamaemelum nobile

CHAMOMILE

Family Compositae

Leaves Evergreen. An herbaceous perennial. Alternate. Entire. Finely dissected. Each segment linear and pubescent. Bright green. Aromatic. Leaves to 2 inches long. Each segment to 1/8 inch in length. Stems light green and pubescent.

Flowers Yellow. The heads are to one inch across. On stems which are to one foot long. Some flowers are buttonlike. Others have the typical daisy flower, with the disk flowers being yellow and the ray ones white. Summer.

Fruit A 3-angled, smooth achene.

Environment Full sun best, but tolerant to partial shade. Not tolerant to foot traffic, to hot summer winds, cold winds. To zero degrees or lower.

Pests Soil Mealybug. Slugs. Snails.

Propagation Seed. Division. Self-sows.

Rate of Growth Moderate

Pruning Can be rolled and mowed, to keep flatter and more compact.

Seasonal Value Foliage. Flowers. Fragrance (Foliage).

Shape Mat-forming

Spread Wide

Height 3 to 6 inches

Soil Tolerant to drought and to some alkalinity. A light, well-drained soil is best. Keep on the dry side.

Use Ground cover. Borders. Between stepping stones. Rock gardens. The flowers are used medicinally and the dried ones for a tea.

Origin Africa. Azores.

Comments Was once *Anthemis nobilis*. It came to America with the early settlers. Has naturalized, to become a weed in many parts of the United States. Has been a turf substitute in European gardens since the middle ages. Also used as a blonde hair rinse.

74

Chlorophytum comosum

SPIDER PLANT

Family Liliaceae

Leaves Evergreen. An herbaceous perennial. Alternate and tufted. Basal. Mostly entire. Linear to lanceolate. Grasslike. Glabrous and glandular-dotted both sides. Parallel-veined, being especially conspicuous below. Medium green above. Glaucous below. 12 to 18 inches long. To 3/4 inch in width.

Flowers White or greenish. To 3/4 inch across. In loose panicles which protrude above the foliage. Regular. Perianth of 6 segments. Stamens 6. Fall-winter.

Fruit A 3-angled capsule.

Environment Partial shade best. Tolerant to considerable shade. Will grow indoors. To 20 degrees.

Pests Caterpillars. Slugs. Snails.

Propagation Seed. Division.

Rate of Growth Rapid

Pruning Remove dead flowers. Keep under control. Aggressive. Spreads by rhizomes and stolons, with new plants forming on the latter. Roots tuberous.

Seasonal Value Foliage. Flowers. Fall color (Flowers).

Shape Clumping. Trailing.

Spread Wide

Height 1 to 3 feet

Soil Best with sufficient organic matter and moisture.

Use Ground cover. Hanging baskets. Indoors.

Origin South Africa

Comments *Chlorophytum* means green plant. *comosum* means tufted, or with hair in tufts. Former names include *Anthericum comosum, A. elatum, Asphadelus capensis, Chlorophytum capense, C. elatum* and *C. sternbergianum.* The variegated cultivars include 'Mandaianum', 'Picturatum', 'Variegatum' and 'Vittatum'.

Chorizema cordatum

HEART-LEAF FLAME PEA
AUSTRALIAN FLAME PEA

Family Leguminosae

Leaves Evergreen. Alternate. With prickly teeth. Cordate to ovate or lanceolate. Revolute. Pubescent and glandular-dotted both sides. Coriaceous. Medium to dark green. One inch or more in length. Nearly as wide. Stems hairy.

Flowers Orange-red, with purplish wing petals. Each 1/2 to 3/4 inch across. Mostly in terminal racemes which are to 6 inches long. Irregular. Petals 5. Stamens 10. Stems hairy. Early spring-summer.

Fruit An ovoid, short legume.

Environment Full sun or partial shade. Probably best in the latter. Better flower color in some shade. To 24 degrees.

Pests Aphids. Thrips.

Propagation Seed. Cuttings.

Rate of Growth Rapid

Pruning Can be cut back for more compactness and for desired shape. Do this after flowering.

Seasonal Value Foliage. Flowers.

Shape Sprawling

Spread 3 to 5 feet or more.

Height 3 to 5 feet or more.

Soil Tolerant to soils and to drought, but best with some water.

Use Ground cover. Containers. Over walls.

Origin Australia

Comments Sometimes incorrectly named *C. illicifolium*, but the latter grows only from 2 to 3 feet in height.

Cistus salvifolius

Family Cistaceae

Leaves Evergreen. Opposite. Entire. Elliptic to oblong. Conspicuously veined. Stellate-tomentose both sides. Scabrous. Rugose above. Not undulated. Grayish-green. Aromatic. 1 3/4 inches long. About 3/4 to one inch in width.

Flowers White, with yellow spots at base of petals. From one to 1 1/2 or 2 inches across. Profuse. Solitary,or several together. Regular. Petals 5. Stamens numerous. Late spring.

Fruit A dry, dehiscent, 5-angled capsule.

Environment Full sun or partial shade. Tolerant to seaside conditions, including winds, salt spray. Also tolerant to desert conditions. To 15 degrees.

Pests Aphids

Propagation Seed. Cuttings.

Rate of Growth Rapid

Pruning As needed.

Seasonal Value Foliage. Flowers. Fragrance (Foliage).

Shape Sprawling

Spread To 6 feet

Height To 2 feet

Soil Tolerant to soils and to drought. Good drainage important.

Use Ground cover. Erosion control. Slopes

Origin Southern Europe

Comments Was once *C. villosus 'Prostratus'*. Is said to be fire-resistant.

Clivia miniata

Family Amaryllidaceae

Leaves Evergreen. An herbaceous perennial. Alternate and basal. 2-ranked. Entire. Broadly linear. Revolute. Parallel-veined. Midvein not prominent. Glabrous and glandular-dotted both sides. Dark glossy green. Straplike. To 2 1/2 feet long and to 2 inches wide.

Flowers Scarlet, with a yellowish coloring inside. Funnelform. 2 to 3 inches long and as wide. In a terminal umbel on a solid scape. 12 to 20-flowered. Regular. Not fragrant. Perianth 6-lobed. Stamens usually 6. From December to April, or longer.

Fruit A globose, pulpy, red berry.

Environment Partial shade. Tolerant to considerable shade. Best in a protected area. Will grow indoors. To about 40 degrees.

Pests Slugs. Snails.

Propagation Seed. Division.

Rate of Growth Moderate to slow

Pruning Remove old flowers and leaves. Tuberous-rooted. Spreads somewhat.

Seasonal Value Foliage. Flowers. Winter color (Flowers).

Shape Clumping

Spread 1 1/2 to 2 feet

Height 1 1/2 to 2 feet

Soil Best if fertile, moist and with good drainage. Responds to fertilizing during the growing period.

Use Ground cover. Containers. Indoors.

Origin South Africa

Comments Formerly *Imantophyllum miniatum. miniata* means cinnabar-red. Plant with top of bulb just above soil level. Allow to rest from fall to early winter. May flower better in a container if somewhat pot-bound. The Belgian and French hybrids have yellow to deep orange-red flowers on thick leaves. The Zimmerman hybrids have white flowers and/or with shades of orange, red or yellow.

Convolvulus cneorum

Family Convolvulaceae

Leaves Evergreen. Alternate or whorled. Entire. Lanceolate to spatulate. With a conspicuous midrib. White-tomentose both sides. 1/2 to 2 1/2 inches long. 1/4 to 3/8 inch or more in width. Stems brownish and white-tomentose.

Flowers White, tinted with pink. Funnelform and terminal. In loose clusters. One to 6 flowers to a cluster. Each 1 1/2 to 2 inches across. Regular. Petals 5. Stamens 5. May-September.

Fruit A globose, 2-celled capsule.

Environment Full sun best, where it is usually more compact. To 20 degrees.

Pests Black Scale. Mites. Nematodes.

Propagation Seed. Cuttings.

Rate of Growth Moderate to rapid

Pruning Only as needed to make more compact.

Seasonal Value Foliage. Flowers.

Shape Compact. Rounded.

Spread 2 to 4 feet

Height 2 to 4 feet

Soil Best on the dry side. Provide good drainage. Drought-tolerant.

Use Ground cover. Borders. Group plantings. Rock gardens. Slopes.

Origin Southern Europe

Comments *Convolvulus* means to entwine. Some species have this characteristic. Some species are noxious weeds, difficult to control. The plant is said to be fire-resistant.

Convolvulus sabatius

Family Convolvulaceae

Leaves Evergreen. An herbaceous perennial. May become woody. Alternate. Entire. Orbicular to ovate. With conspicuous veins. Glandular-dotted and pubescent both sides. Ciliate. Grayish-green. 1/2 to 1 1/2 inches across and about as long. The stems are slender, hairy and glandular-dotted.

Flowers Lavender-blue. One to 2 inches across. In one to 6-flowered clusters. Regular. Gamopetalous. Stamens 5. Funnelform. Opening only in the morning and closing in the shade. June-November.

Fruit A 4-valved capsule.

Environment Full sun. To 15 degrees

Pests Aphids

Propagation Seed. Cuttings. Self-sows.

Rate of Growth Moderate to rapid

Pruning Thin as needed. Cut back in the winter period.

Seasonal Value Foliage. Flowers.

Shape Mounding

Spread To 3 feet or more.

Height One to 2 feet

Soil Gravelly soil best. Good drainage important. Drought-tolerant.

Use Ground cover. Hanging baskets. Raised beds. Slopes. Over walls.

Origin North Africa

Comments Formerly *C. mauritanicus*

Coprosma kirkii

Family   Rubiaceae

Leaves   Evergreen. Opposite. Entire. Oblong to oblanceolate. With a conspicuous midrib. Glabrous both sides. Medium to yellowish-green. To 1 1/2inches long. About 1/4 inch wide. The margins are somewhat reddish. Stems are stiff and pubescent.

Flowers   White. About 1/2 inch across. Funnelform. Solitary or in cymes. Regular. Dioecious. Corolla 4 to 5-lobed. Stamens 4 to 5.

Fruit   A bluish, red-speckled, translucent, oblong drupe. Usually 2-celled.

Environment   Full sun or partial shade. Tolerant to salt spray and to seaside conditions. To about 20 or 30 degrees.

Pests   Apparently few.

Propagation   Seed. Cuttings. Layering.

Rate of Growth   Moderate

Pruning   Tolerant. Head back periodically as needed.

Seasonal Value   Foliage

Shape   Stiff

Spread   To 10 feet or more.

Height   2 to 3 feet

Soil   Tolerant to soils and to drought. Best with good drainage.

Use   Ground cover. Containers. Erosion control. Slopes. Over walls.

Origin   New Zealand. Is a cross between C. acerosa and C. repens.

Comments   At one time was *C. microphylla*. The word *Coprosma* refers to the supposedly fetid odor of the plants. Some species of *Coprosma* have been used in dyeing. There are over 90 species in the Pacific region. Over 45 are native to New Zealand. In those areas at least, the fruit is very conspicuous and much desired by birds.

Coreopsis auriculata 'Nana'

DWARF COREOPSIS
DWARF TICKSEED

Family Compositae

Leaves Evergreen or semi-evergreen. An herbaceous perennial. Alternate. Entire. Often with one or two basal lobes. Ovate to lanceolate. Usually pubescent below, glabrous above. Ciliate. Medium green. 2 to 5 inches long. To one inch or more in width. Petioles reddish at the base.

Flowers Yellow. In heads which are 1 1/2 to 2 inches across. Profuse. Solitary on long stems. Regular. Corolla 4 to 5-lobed. Stamens 4 or 5. Spring to fall.

Fruit Winged achenes. Seed attractive to birds.

Environment Full sun. To 20 or 30 degrees. If too cold will be deciduous.

Pests Aphids. Mites. Soil Mealybug.

Propagation Seed. Cuttings. Division. Self-sows.

Rate of Growth Moderate to rapid

Pruning Keep under control. Spreads by stolons. Remove dead flowers to encourage new ones.

Seasonal Value Foliage. Flowers.

Shape Mat-forming

Spread 2 to 3 feet

Height 5 to 6 inches

Soil Tolerant to soils and to drought, but best with some water.

Use Ground cover. Rock gardens.

Origin Virginia to Florida and Mississippi.

Comments *Coreopsis* means buglike. *auriculata* means with ears.

Correa pulchella

Family Rutaceae

Leaves Evergreen. Opposite. Entire. Ovate to oblong. Mature leaves mostly glabrous above, stellate-hairy below. Glandular-dotted both sides. Ciliate, with stellate hairs. Dark green above, grayish-green below. Appearing grayish. Undulate. To 1 1/2 inches long. To 1/2 inch wide. Stems pinkish and hairy.

Flowers Pink. Each from 3/4 to one inch long. About 1/4 inch across. Tubular or campanulate. Pendulous. Regular. Petals 4. Stamens 8. November-April.

Fruit A capsule which dehisces into 4 sections, each with one or 2 seeds.

Environment Full sun in coastal areas. Partial shade where warm. Tolerant to salt air, but protect from strong winds. To 20 or 30 degrees.

Pests Apparently few.

Propagation Cuttings

Rate of Growth Moderate

Pruning Can be headed somewhat following bloom; however, will break poorly from old wood.

Seasonal Value Foliage. Flowers. Winter color (Flowers).

Shape Round to sprawling

Spread 6 to 8 feet

Height To 3 feet

Soil Tolerant to poor soils and to some drought. Not tolerant to excess water or to fertilizing. Provide good drainage.

Use Ground cover. Containers. Raised beds. Slopes. Specimen.

Origin Australia

Comments Previous names include *C. neglecta* and *C. speciosa*. This plant is the *Correa* most used in California at the present time.

Cotoneaster dammeri

BEARBERRY COTONEASTER

Family Rosaceae

Leaves Evergreen. Alternate. Entire. Elliptic, oblong, oval or obovate. Coriaceous. Conspicuously-veined. Glabrous and dark glossy green above. White-pubescent below. Revolute. Acute to emarginate. Turning reddish in the winter. From 1/2 to over one inch long. To 1/2 inch wide. Stems brownish and sparsely hairy.

Flowers White. Each to 1/2 inch across. Usually borne singly. Regular. With 5 rounded petals. Stamens about 20. Early summer.

Fruit A brilliant red, globose pome. To 1/4 inch across. Fall.

Environment Full sun or partial shade. To below zero.

Pests Aphids. Black Scale. Lacebug, Thrips. Woolly Apple Aphid. Mites. Fire Blight.

Propagation Usually by cuttings, by division or layering.

Rate of Growth Moderate to rapid

Pruning Tolerant, if needed.

Seasonal Value Foliage. Flowers. Fruit. Fall color (Fruit, leaves).

Shape Prostrate, with trailing branches.

Spread To 10 feet

Height 3 to 6 inches

Soil Tolerant to soils and to drought. Provide good drainage. Best if somewhat on the dry side.

Use Ground cover. Erosion control. Rock gardens. Over walls.

Origin Central China

Comments Formerly *C. humifusus* and *C. dammeri* var. *radicans*. The cultivars include 'Coral Beauty', 'Royal Beauty', 'Lowfast' and 'Skogholmen'.

95

Cotoneaster horizontalis

Family Rosaceae

Leaves Evergreen to deciduous. If deciduous, only for a short time. Alternate. Entire. Nearly orbicular. Mucronate. Midrib conspicuous. Glabrous, bright glossy green and glandular-dotted above. Pubescent below. Ciliate. Good fall coloring. To 1/2 inch long. Nearly as wide. Stems hairy and brownish when mature.

Flowers White to pinkish. Each to 3/16 inch across. Solitary or in cymose clusters. After the leaves reappear. Regular. Petals 5. Stamens about 20. Late spring-summer.

Fruit Red berries. (Pomes.) Usually with 2 seeds. To 3/16 inch across. Fall-winter.

Environment Full sun best. Tolerant to some shade, also to wind. To zero degrees.

Pests Aphids, including Woolly Apple Aphid. Black Scale. Lacebug. Thrips. Mites. Fire Blight.

Propagation Seeds. Cuttings. Layering.

Rate of Growth Moderate to rapid

Pruning Tolerant if needed.

Seasonal Value Foliage. Flowers. Fruit. Fall and winter coloring (Fruit and foliage).

Shape Stiff, with arching branches

Spread To 15 feet

Height To 3 feet

Soil Tolerant to soils and to drought. Usually best on the dry side.

Use Ground cover. Bonsai. Erosion control. Espalier. Low barrier. Slopes. Specimen. Over walls.

Orign West China

Comments Cotoneaster means quincelike, referring to the leaves of some species. At one time, this plant was named *C. davidianus*. Cultivars include 'Minor', 'Praecox', 'Prostratus', 'Robustus', 'Variegatus' and 'Wilsonii'.

96

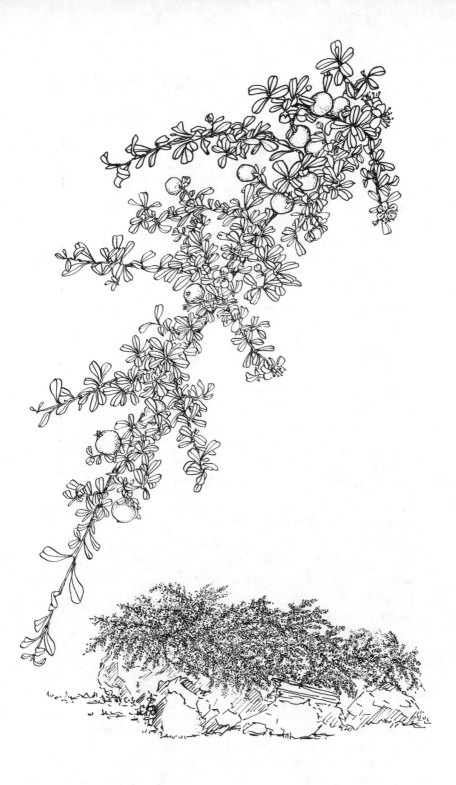

97

Cotoneaster microphyllus

ROCKSPRAY COTONEASTER

Family Rosaceae

Leaves Evergreen. Alternate. Entire. Obovate to oblong. Obtuse, Revolute. Midrib conspicuous. Glabrous above, gray-tomentose below. Dark, glossy green. To 1/2 inch long. About 1/4 inch wide. Stems are glabrous and grayish-brown.

Flowers White. Usually solitary, but sometimes 2 to 3 at the ends of lateral branches. Each about 3/8 inch across. Regular. Petals 5. Stamens about 20. Late spring-summer.

Fruit Rosy red berry (pome). Usually solitary. 1/4 inch across. Fall-winter.

Environment Full sun to partial shade. Tolerant to seacoast conditions. To below zero.

Pests Aphids, including Woolly Apple Aphid. Black Scale. Lacebug. Thrips. Fire Blight.

Propagation Cuttings. Self-layering.

Rate of Growth Moderate

Pruning Usually requires very little.

Seasonal Value Foliage. Flowers. Fall color (Fruit).

Shape Compact. Prostrate. Stiff.

Spread To 6 feet or more.

Height 2 to 3 feet

Soil Tolerant to soils and to drought. Usually best if somewhat neglected. Do not overwater.

Use Ground cover. Erosion control. Rock gardens. Slopes. Over walls.

Origin Himalayas. West China.

Comments Cultivars include 'Cochleatus' and 'Emerald Spray'. *C. m. var. thymifolius* is even more compact, with flowers 2 to 4 in a cluster. Also, the leaves are smaller.

Cyclamen persicum

Family Primulaceae

Leaves Evergreen. An herbaceous perennial. Basal. Crenate. Cordate or orbicular. Somewhat revolute. Veins conspicuous, being whitish above and reddish below. Glabrous and glandular-dotted both sides. Dark green above, pinkish below. 3 inches or more across and as long. Petioles are pinkish and long.

Flowers Pink, red or white. 2 to 3 inches across. Somewhat resembling shooting stars. Not fragrant. Regular. Corolla 5-lobed. Stamens 5. From fall through spring, or longer.

Fruit A 5-valved capsule.

Environment Partial shade, in a protected area. 25 to 30 degrees.

Pests Aphids. Cyclamen Mite. Thrips. Botrytis. Cyclamen Stunt.

Propagation Seed. Tubers.

Rate of Growth Slow, especially from seed.

Pruning Remove dead flowers and foliage.

Seasonal Value Foliage. Flowers. Fall coloring (Flowers).

Shape Mounding

Spread 10 to 12 inches

Height 10 to 12 inches

Soil Fertile, acid and moist. Provide good drainage.

Use Ground cover. Containers. Indoors.

Origin East Mediterranean region.

Comments The flowers of this species are usually larger than those of other species. This plant was once *C. indicum* and *C. vernalis*. The tuber has been used medicinally. There are many cultivars. Plant with the top portion of the tuber above ground.

Cymbalaria muralis

KENILWORTH IVY

Family Scrophulariaceae

Leaves Evergreen. An herbaceous perennial. Mostly alternate. 3 to 7-lobed. Cordate to orbicular or reniform. Palmately veined. Glabrous and glandular-dotted both sides and on stems. Medium green. 1/2 to one inch across and about as long. Stems somewhat striated.

Flowers Blue, with a yellow throat. Solitary and axillary. 3/8 inch long and about as much across. Irregular. Corolla 4 to 5-lobed. Stamens 4. Summer-fall, or longer.

Fruit A capsule

Environment Partial shade usually best. To below zero. However, may die down with cold, to reappear with warmer weather.

Pests Aphids. Mites. Snails. Slugs.

Propagation Seed. Division.

Rate of Growth Rapid

Pruning Keep under control. Invasive. Spreads by stolons.

Seasonal Value Foliage. Flowers.

Shape Prostrate. Trailing.

Spread Wide

Height 2 to 3 inches

Soil Best when fertile and moist.

Use Ground cover. Hanging baskets. In terrariums. On and over walls.

Origin Europe

Comments Formerly *Linaria cymbalaria* and *Antirrhinum cymbalaria*. *Cymbalaria* means cymbal. This plant is much naturalized. *C. aequitriloba* is a species that is much more compact and lower-growing.

102

Daphne cneorum

GARLAND DAPHNE
GARLAND FLOWER

Family   Thymelaceae

Leaves   Evergreen. Alternate. Entire. Narrowly oblong to oblanceolate. Cuneate. Mucronulate. Coriaceous. Midrib conspicuous. Dark glossy green above. Glaucous below. Glabrous and glandular-dotted both sides. 1/2 to one inch long. 1/8 to 1/4 inch wide. Stems brownish and somewhat hairy.

Flowers   Rosy pink to white. Each to 3/8 inch across. In dense terminal heads. Many-flowered. Sessile. Very fragrant. Regular. Stamens 8. April-May.

Fruit   A yellowish-brown drupe.

Environment   Full sun in cool areas. Partial shade where warm. To below zero.

Pests   Thrips. Crown Rot. Leaf Spot.

Propagation   Cuttings

Rate of Growth   Moderate

Pruning   Only as needed.

Seasonal Value   Foliage. Flowers. Fragrance (Flowers).

Shape   Mounding

Spread   To 3 feet

Height   To one foot

Soil   Best in a fairly good soil, with good drainage. Needs sufficient moisture. Mulching is helpful.

Use   Ground cover. Containers. Rock gardens.

Origin   Europe

Comments   The bark, when crushed, has been used to stupefy fish. Varieties and cultivars include the following: *var. pygmaea*. 'Albo-Marginata', 'Alba', 'Major', 'Ruby Glow'.

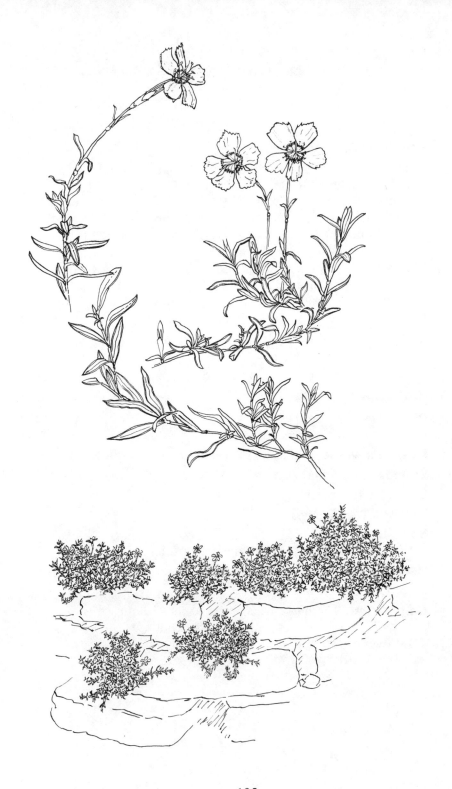

Dianthus deltoides

MAIDEN PINK

Family Caryophyllaceae

Leaves Evergreen. An herbaceous perennial. Opposite. Often 4-ranked. Entire. Linear to oblanceolate. Glabrous above. Stiff-hairy on midvein below. Glandular-dotted both sides. Ciliate. Medium green or glaucous. 1/2 inch long. To 1/4 inch wide. 3-nerved. Stems reddish and hairy.

Flowers Light lavender. 3/4 inch across. Solitary. Terminal. With a dark, v-shaped band at the base of each petal. Fragrant. Regular. Petals 5. Stamens 10. Spring and summer and again in the fall.

Fruit A cylindrical, oblong to ovoid, 4-valved capsule.

Environment Full sun or partial shade. The latter especially where hot. To below zero.

Pests Aphids. Mites. Fusarium. Rust.

Propagation Seed. Cuttings. Division. Layering.

Rate of Growth Moderate to slow.

Pruning Remove dead flowers for prolonged bloom. Keep under control. Spreads by stolons.

Seasonal Value Foliage. Flowers. Fragrance (Flowers).

Shape Mat-forming

Spread Wide

Height 6 to 18 inches

Soil Fertile. With good drainage. Best if not acid. Drought tolerant.

Use Ground cover. Borders. Cut flowers. Rock gardens. Over walls.

Origin Europe

Comments *deltòides* here means with a v-shaped pattern in the throat of the flower. The many cultivars include 'Albus', 'Coccineus', 'Compactus', 'Erectus', 'Glaucus', 'Nanus', 'Roseus', 'Ruber', 'Splendens', 'Serpyllifolius', 'Vampire', 'Zing', 'Zing Rose'.

Dichondra micrantha

Family   Convolvulaceae

Leaves   Evergreen. An herbaceous perennial. Alternate. Entire. Orbicular or cordate to reniform. With conspicuous veining. Nearly glabrous above. Pubescent below. Glandular-dotted both sides. Dark green. 1/2 to one inch in width and about as long. Stems are weak and pubescent.

Flowers   Greenish-yellow. Very small. Each about 1/8 inch across. Solitary and axillary. Regular. Corolla gamopetalous. Stamens 5.

Fruit   A one-seeded, 2-lobed capsule, about 1/8 inch across.

Environment   Full or partial shade. Usually better color in some shade. To 35 degrees.

Pests   Cutworms. Dichondra Flea Beetle. Lucerne Moth. Vegetable Weevil. Mites. Nematodes. Slugs. Snails. Rhizoctonia. Sclerotium rolfsii.

Propagation   Seed. Division. Self-sows.

Rate of Growth   Moderate

Pruning   Keep under control. Spreads by stolons and by seed.

Seasonal Value   Foliage

Shape   Mat-forming

Spread   Wide

Height   3 to 6 inches

Soil   Best when fertile, with sufficient organic matter, moisture and with good drainage.

Use   Ground cover. Between stepping stones.

Origin   China. Japan. Mexico. Texas. West Indies.

Comments   Formerly *D. carolinensis* and *D. repens*. *Dichondra* means double and grain, referring to the shape of the fruit.

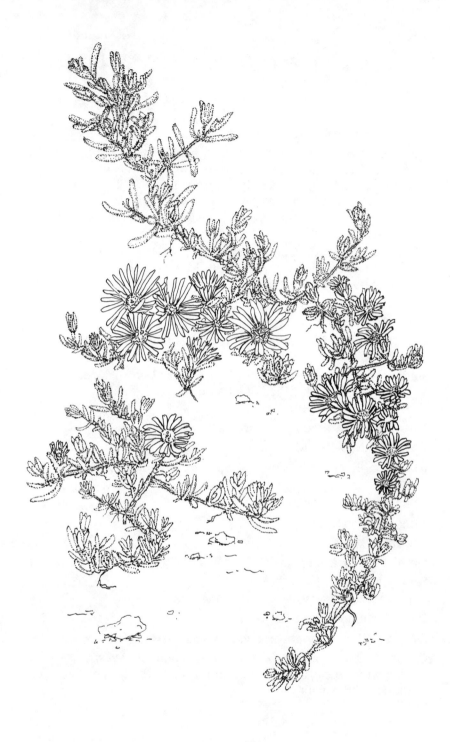

109

Drosanthemum floribundum

Family Aizoaceae

Leaves Evergreen. An herbaceous perennial. Opposite or whorled or fascicled. Entire. Terete to 3-angled. Glabrous. With conspicuously glistening dots (papillae). Grayish. To 1/2 inch long. 1/8 inch wide. Stems terete, white hairy. Sometimes woody.

Flowers Pale Pink. To 3/4 inch across. Solitary or in threes. Regular. Petals numerous. Stamens numerous. Spring and summer.

Fruit A 4 to 5-valved capsule.

Environment Full sun. Good in coastal areas. 25 to 30 degrees.

Pests Aphids. Mealybug. Scales.

Propagation Seed. Cuttings. Self-layering.

Rate of Growth Rapid

Pruning Keep under control. Spreads by stolons. Remove dead flowers to encourage more bloom.

Seasonal Value Foliage. Flowers.

Shape Decumbent. Trailing.

Spread Wide

Height 6 inches

Soil Tolerant to soils and to drought, but better with some water.

Use Ground cover. Erosion control. Slopes. Hanging baskets. Indoors. Over walls.

Origin South Africa

Comments Said to be the best Ice Plant for use on steep slopes. Fire-resistant if watered periodically. The name *Drosanthemum* refers to the fact that the flowers are similar to those of the plant Drosera. *D. hispidum* grows to 2 feet in height and to 3 feet across. *D. speciosum* has orange flowers with green centers.

Duchesnea indica

Family Rosaceae

Leaves Evergreen. An herbaceous perennial. Alternate. Palmately compound, with three crenately-toothed leaflets. Each rhombic to ovate or obovate. Pubescent both sides, at least along the veins. Ciliate. Medium green. To one inch long. 1/2 inch wide. Petioles long, hairy and reddish at the base.

Flowers Yellow. Solitary. Each 1/2 inch across. Regular. Petals 5. Stamens 20-25, in groups of 5. Intermittently throughout the year.

Fruit A red, dry and spongy receptacle. Seen above the foliage. Said to be edible, but not very tasty. 1/2 inch across. Attractive to birds.

Environment Usually best in partial shade. Tolerant to sun in cool areas. To below zero.

Pests Aphids. Mites. Rust.

Propagation Seed. Division.

Rate of Growth Rapid

Pruning Keep under control. Very aggressive. Spreads by stolons.

Seasonal Value Foliage. Flowers. Fruit.

Shape Trailing

Spread Wide

Height 3 to 6 inches or more.

Soil Tolerant, but best with sufficient water.

Use Ground cover. Borders. Hanging Baskets. Rock Gardens.

Origin India

Comments *indica* means from India. Was once named *Fragaria indica*. It is often confused with *Fragaria,* however the latter has white flowers. *F. chiloensis* also is white hairy below. *Fragaria* too, at least in California is not subject to Rust whereas *Duchesnea* often is infected with this fungus disease.

Erica herbacea *'Springwood White'*

Family Ericaceae

Leaves Evergreen. Opposite or whorled. Entire. Needlelike or awl-shaped. 2-ranked. Involute. Usually 3-sided. Glabrous and glandular-dotted all sides. Medium green and glossy. Ciliate. About 1/4 inch long. Stems brownish.

Flowers White or cream-colored. Each about 1/4 inch long. Solitary or in axillary pairs. In upright, terminal, one-sided racemes which are one to 2 inches long. Corolla urn-shaped. With 4 lobes. Regular. Stamens usually 8. January-April.

Fruit A 4-valved capsule, with many seeds.

Environment Full sun or partial shade. Some shade where warm. Does well in coastal areas. To below zero.

Pests Aphids. Black Scale. Greedy Scale. Phytophthora. Mildew. Attractive to bees.

Propagation Cuttings

Rate of Growth Rapid

Pruning Remove dead flowers. Shape as needed.

Seasonal Value Foliage. Flowers. Winter color (Flowers).

Shape Stiff. Upright. Rounded.

Spread To one foot

Height To one foot

Soil Tolerant to heavy soils, acidity and to some alkalinity. Needs sufficient moisture but requires good drainage.

Use Ground cover. Containers.

Origin Europe

Comments The parent plant was once *E. carnea* and *E. mediterranea*. There are many cultivars from the parent. Flowers may vary in these from pink and purple to red and white.

Erigeron karvinskianus

Family Compositae

Leaves Evergreen. An herbaceous perennial. Alternate. Mostly entire, but often toothed or lobed at the apex. Lancolate, elliptic or obovate. Glandular-dotted and pubescent both sides. Ciliate. Medium green. To one inch or more in length. To 1/2 inch wide.

Flowers With white rays that fade to pink. Purplish on the underside. In heads which are to 3/4 inch across. With yellow centers. Regular. Corolla 5-lobed. Stamens 4 to 5. Spring - most of the year.

Fruit An achene

Environment Full sun or partial shade. To 15 or 20 degrees.

Pests Aphids

Propagation Seed. Cuttings. Division.

Rate of Growth Rapid once established.

Pruning Remove dead flowers. Keep under control. Aggressive.

Seasonal Value Foliage. Flowers.

Shape Low. Trailing.

Spread Wide

Height To 12 inches or more.

Soil Tolerant, but best if light. Drought tolerant, but best with some water. Provide good drainage.

Use Ground cover. Borders. Containers. Hanging Baskets. Rock gardens.

Origin Mexico to Venezuela.

Comments Was once named *E. mucronatus* and also *Vittadinia triloba*. *Erigeron* means old man in the spring, referring to the fact that some species are densely white hairy, especially early in the season.

Erodium chamaedryoides

Family Geraniaceae

Leaves Evergreen. An herbaceous perennial. Mostly basal. Crenate. Orbicular to ovate. Somewhat cordate. Pubescent both sides. Medium to dark green. To 1/2 inch long. About as wide. Stems hairy and somewhat reddish.

Flowers White to pink. With pinkish veining. To 1/2 inch across. Each peduncle with one flower. Regular. Petals 5. Stamens 5. April-October.

Fruit A beaked capsule, with a twisted tail. To 5/8 inch long.

Environment Full sun or partial shade. To 5 or 10 degrees.

Pests Aphids. Soil Mealybug.

Propagation Seed. Cuttings. Division.

Rate of Growth Moderate to slow

Pruning Remove old flowers to encourage the new.

Seasonal Value Foliage. Flowers.

Shape Tufting.

Spread To 12 inches

Height 3 to 6 inches

Soil Tolerant, to a fairly dry, well-drained soil, but best with some moisture.

Use Ground cover. Alpine gardens. Rock gardens. Over walls.

Origin Balearic Islands and Corsica

Comments *Erodium* means Heron's bill, referring to the fruiting structure. The species name refers to the Oak-like leaves. The common name refers to the fruit appearance. This plant was once named *Geranium chamaedryoides*. Cultivars include 'Album' and 'Roseum'. The latter may be *E. corsicum*.

118

119

Erysimum kotschyanum

Family Cruciferae

Leaves Evergreen. An herbaceous perennial. Alternate. Toothed. Linear to oblanceolate or spatulate. Midrib conspicuous. Hairy and glandular-dotted both sides. Sparsely ciliate. Medium to darker green. To 1 1/2 inches long. About 1/4 inch wide.

Flowers Bright yellow. To 1/2 inch across. In racemes. Fragrant. Regular. Petals 4. Stamens 6. Spring and summer.

Fruit A linear, 2-celled silique. About one inch long.

Environment Full sun. To zero degrees.

Pests Aphids. Mites. Soil Mealybug.

Propagation Seed. Cuttings. Division.

Rate of Growth Rapid

Pruning Keep under control. Spreads by stolons.

Seasonal Value Foliage. Flowers.

Shape Tufting. Mat-forming.

Spread Wide

Height 3 to 6 inches

Soil Tolerant to soils and to drought, but best with some water.

Use Ground cover. Rock gardens.

Origin Asia Minor

Comments *Erysimum* means for drawing blisters, referring to the medicinal properties of this plant.

Euonymus fortunei var. radicans

COMMON WINTER CREEPER
TRAILING EUONYMUS

Family Celastraceae

Leaves Evergreen. Opposite. Usually crenate to serrate. Elliptic to ovate. Mostly glabrous. With whitish dots above and glandular-dotted below. Coriaceous. Glossy dark green. With whitish veins. Winter color reddish to purplish. One to 2 inches long. To one inch in width. Stems with white dots, often squarish, and producing holdfasts.

Flowers Greenish-white or purplish. Small. In axillary cymes. Petals 4 or 5. Stamens 4 or 5. Regular. Summer.

Fruit Pale pink capsules. With 3 to 5 valves. Nearly globose. Opening in the fall to reveal the orange seeds. Capsules about 1/3 inch across.

Environment Full sun to partial shade. Better fall coloring in the sun. Tolerant to wind and to below zero and to considerable shade.

Pests Aphids. Euonymus and Greedy Scale. Thrips. Mildew.

Propagation Cuttings. Division. Layering.

Rate of Growth Fairly slow to start. Slower in shade.

Pruning Thin as needed. Keep under control.

Seasonal Value Foliage. Fruit (Fall).

Shape Procumbent, or a vine.

Spread Wide

Height To one foot. To 20 feet as a vine.

Soil Tolerant to soils and to drought.

Use Ground cover. Erosion control. Vine.

Origin Japan. South Korea.

Comments Was once *E. japonica var. radicans*. Also the genus was sometimes spelled *Evonymus*. There are many cultivars. The wood of some species has been used in woodworking. Also, the bark of one species has been used medicinally.

Felicia amelloides

BLUE MARGUERITE
BLUE DAISY

Family Compositae

Leaves Evergreen. An herbaceous perennial. Opposite. Entire. Oblong to obovate or elliptic. 3-veined from base, especially conspicuously so below. Mostly glabrous above. Sparsely hairy below. Glandular-dotted both sides. Ciliate. To 1 1/4 inches long. About 1/2 inch wide. Stems glandular-dotted and hairy.

Flowers Ray flowers are an intense blue. Stamens are yellow. In heads. On long peduncles. Solitary. To 1 1/4 inches across. Regular. Corolla 4 to 5-lobed. Stamens 5. All summer, into the fall, and sometimes longer.

Fruit A glabrous achene.

Environment Full sun to partial shade. To 20 degrees.

Pests Aphids. Mildew.

Propagation Seed. Cuttings. Self-sowing.

Rate of Growth Moderate to rapid

Pruning Remove dead flowers to stimulate more bloom. Keep under control.

Seasonal Value Foliage. Flowers.

Shape Sprawling

Spread 4 to 5 feet

Height 1 1/2 to 3 feet

Soil Drought-tolerant but best with some water. Tolerant to soils, but needs good drainage.

Use Ground cover. Containers. Cut flowers. Over walls.

Origin South Africa

Comments Formerly named *F. aethiopica* and also *Agathaea coelestis*. There are many cultivars, including 'Astrid Thomas', 'Blue Gabriel', 'George Lewis', 'Jolly', 'Martha Chandler', 'Midnight', 'Rhapsody in Blue', 'Santa Anita', 'San Gabriel' and 'San Luis'.

Festuca ovina var. glauca

Family Gramineae

Leaves Evergreen. An herbaceous perennial. Basal. Grasslike. Involute. Entire. Glabrous. Bluish-gray. 6 to 8 inches long.

Flowers Brownish when mature. Spikelets mostly 4 to 6-flowered. In a panicle which is often one-sided and is to 6 inches long. Stamens one to 3. Summer.

Fruit A grain.

Environment Full sun to partial shade. To below zero.

Pests Soil Mealybug

Propagation Seed. Division.

Rate of Growth Moderate to rapid

Pruning Cut back occasionally. Divide periodically. Remove the dead flowers.

Seasonal Value Foliage. Inflorescence.

Shape Tufted. Mounding.

Spread 12 to 18 inches

Height 6 to 12 inches or more.

Soil Tolerant to soils and to drought, but best with some water.

Use Ground cover. Borders. Planters. Dry arrangements. Rock gardens.

Origin Europe

Comments Was once *F. vulgaris*. *Festuca* is an old name for a grass. *ovina* pertains to sheep. This plant is a bunch grass. It does not form rhizomes or stolons.

126

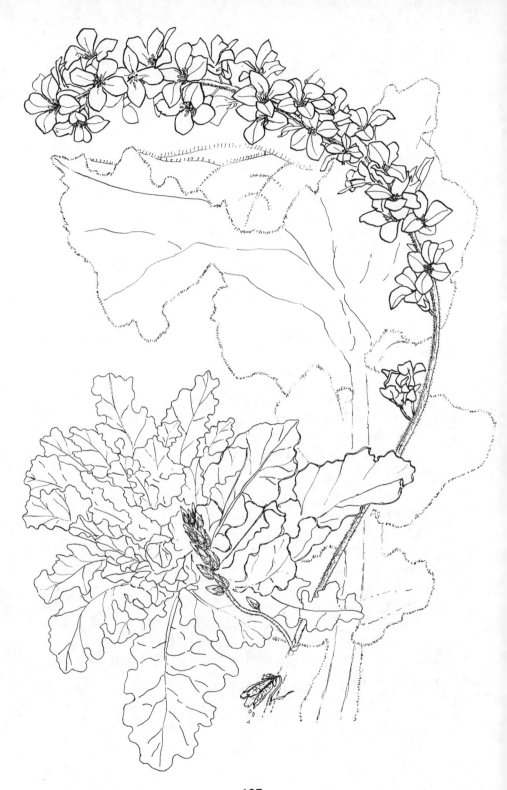

127

Francoa ramosa

Family   Saxifragaceae

Leaves   Evergreen. An herbaceous perennial. Alternate and basal. Crenate to dentate. Lyrate. Broadly oblanceolate. Glabrous above. Hairy on veins below. Glandular-dotted both sides. Medium green. 6 to 12 inches long. 2 to 3 inches wide. Ciliate. Stems hairy.

Flowers   White. Each to 3/4 inch across. In dense, terminal racemes which are 4 to 8 inches long. Stems are 2 to 3 feet long. Regular. Petals 4. Stamens 8. Summer.

Fruit   An oblong, 4-celled and 4-angled capsule. 3/8 to 1/2 inch long.

Environment   Partial shade best. Tolerant to considerable shade and to 15 or 20 degrees.

Pests   Aphids. Soil Mealybug. Slugs. Snails.

Propagation   Seed. Division.

Rate of Growth   Moderate to rapid

Pruning   Remove dead flowers. Keep under control. Has thick rhizomes.

Seasonal Value   Foliage. Flowers.

Shape   Sprawling, clumping.

Spread   2 to 3 feet

Height   One to 2 feet or more.

Soil   Tolerant but best with some moisture.

Use   Ground cover. Cut flowers.

Origin   Chile

Comments   Formerly *F. glabrata. ramosa* means branched, referring probably, to the inflorescence.

128

Fuchsia procumbens

Family Onagraceae

Leaves Evergreen. An herbaceous perennial. Alternate. Serrulate. Cordate to ovate. Nearly orbicular. Glabrous and glandular-dotted both sides. Dull green. Somewhat ciliate. To 1/2 or 3/4 inch long. Nearly as wide. Stems slender, brownish.

Flowers The calyx tube is orange-colored. The calyx lobes are dark purple. The anthers are blue. Apetalous. Erect. Solitary and axillary. 5/16 inch long. Regular. Stamens 8. Late summer-fall.

Fruit A red to purplish and glaucous berry. About 1/2 inch across. Winter.

Environemnt Partial shade best. To about 20 degrees.

Pests Aphids. Mites.

Propagation Cuttings. Division.

Rate of Growth Rapid

Pruning Keep under control. Rather aggressive. Spreads by stolons.

Seasonal Value Foliage. Flowers. Fruit. Winter color (Fruit).

Shape Procumbent. Trailing. Mat-forming.

Spread Wide

Height 6 to 12 inches

Soil Best when fertile, with some water and well-drained.

Use Ground cover. Containers. Hanging baskets. Rock gardens.

Origin New Zealand

Comments A very interesting plant for a shaded area. The flowers are attractive, and the fruit is most conspicuous and seemingly out of proportion to the foliage. Apparently this plant is deciduous in its native habitat. At least one source said that it is rare in New Zealand.

Galium odoratum

Family   Rubiaceae

Leaves   Evergreen. An herbaceous perennial. Whorled. Entire. Obovate to oblanceolate. Glabrous and glandular-dotted both sides. With a fringe of hairs at the base of the whorls. Ciliate. Medium green. Aromatic. One to 1 1/2 inches long. 1/4 to 1/2 inch wide. Stems slender, squarish and grooved.

Flowers   White. To 1/4 inch long. Funnelform. In loose, branching cymes. Protruding above the foliage. Regular. Gamopetalous. Corolla 4-lobed. Stamens 4. Spring and summer.

Fruit   2-seeded, 2-lobed, dry and indehiscent.

Environment   Best in partial shade. To below zero.

Pests   Aphids

Propagation   Seed. Cuttings. Division. Self-sowing.

Rate of Growth   Rapid

Pruning   Keep under control. Spreads by rhizomes. Aggressive.

Seasonal Value   Foliage. Flowers. Fragrance (Leaves). The fragrance is as fresh hay or vanilla.

Shape   Low, erect, creeping.

Spread   Wide

Height   6 to 12 inches

Soil   Fertile, with sufficient moisture.

Use   Ground cover. Borders. Herb gardens.

Origin   Asia. Europe. North Africa.

Comments   Formerly known as *Asperula odorata*. *Asperula* means roughish, describing the feel of the leaves. The word *Galium* refers to a plant used in curdling of milk. The dried leaves and stems are used in the manufacture of May Wine and for tea.

Gardenia augusta 'Radicans'

TRAILING GARDENIA

Family Rubiaceae

Leaves Evergreen. Opposite or in whorls of three. Entire. Oblanceolate. Somewhat revolute. Glabrous both sides. Dark glossy green. To 2 inches long. About 1/2 inch wide. The leaves often are streaked with white. Stems rough, brownish.

Flowers White. 1 1/2 to 2 inches across. Solitary or paired. Terminal, or appearing to be axillary. Mostly funnelform. Fragrant. Regular. Corolla 5 to 11-lobed. Stamens 5 to 9. Summer.

Fruit An orange, ovoid berry.

Environment Full sun. Partial shade were warm. To 20 degrees or lower.

Pests Aphids. Mealybug. White Fly. Mites. Nematodes.

Propagation Cuttings

Rate of Growth Moderate

Pruning Remove dead flowers.

Seasonal Value Foliage. Flowers. Fragrance (Flowers).

Shape Sprawling

Spread 2 to 3 feet

Height 6 to 12 inches

Soil Fertile, moist and acid. If chlorotic, may respond to application or Iron Sulfate. Mulching may be helpful for good growth.

Use Ground cover. Containers.

Origin China

Comments Formerly *G. jasminoides 'Radicans'* and *G. radicans*. The flowers of Gardenia are used in making perfume. The fruit is used for a yellow dye.

Gaultheria procumbens

WINTERGREEN
CHECKERBERRY

Family Ericaceae

Leaves Evergreen. Alternate. Slightly toothed. Elliptic to oblong or obovate. Revolute. Glabrous both sides and glandular-dotted below. Dark glossy green above. Coriaceous. Aromatic. To 2 inches long. About 1 1/4 inches wide. Petioles red. The stems are somewhat woody. They are erect and to 6 inches in length.

Flowers White to pink. Solitary and pendulous. About 1/4 inch across. Regular. Corolla 4 to 5-lobed. Stamens 10. Summer to fall.

Fruit A 5-valved capsule enclosed by a scarlet calyx. About 1/4 inch across. Aromatic.

Environment Partial shade. To below zero.

Pests Aphids. Thrips.

Propagation Seed. Cuttings. Division. Layering.

Rate of Growth Moderate

Pruning Keep under control. Spreads by rhizomes.

Seasonal Value Foliage. Flowers. Fragrance (Foliage, Fruit).

Shape Low. Compact. Creeping.

Spread 2 to 3 feet or more.

Height To 6 inches

Soil Acid. Fertile, with sufficient organic matter. Moist. Tolerant to wet soils.

Use Ground cover. For shady, moist areas.

Origin Eastern United States, south to Alabama and Georgia.

Comments Was formerly *G. repens. repens* means creeping. The leaves and the fruit produce a wintergreen flavor. This was the original source of Wintergreen. The source now is *Betula lenta*. Both the leaves and the fruit are edible. Use the leaves when young and tender.

Gazania 'Copper King'

Family   Compositae

Leaves   Evergreen. An herbaceous perennial. Basal. Toothed. Mostly 3 to 9-lobed toward the apex. Oblanceolate. Revolute. Midrib conspicuous below. Tomentose both sides. Glandular-dotted above. Grayish-green above. White below. 6 to 8 inches long. 1/2 inch wide. Segments are one inch or more in length and about 1/4 inch wide.

Flowers   With irridescent yellow-orange and brown ray colors. The base of each ray is reddish-violet in color and flecked with blue and buff. To 3½ inches across. Regular. Corolla 4 to 5-lobed. Stamens 5. Late spring through summer and most of the year. Opening in the sun.

Fruit   An achene

Environment   Full sun. To 20 or 30 degrees

Pests   Aphids. Soil Mealybug. Thrips. Crown Rot

Propagation   Seed. Cuttings. Division.

Rate of Growth   Moderate to rapid

Pruning   Remove dead flowers. Divide periodically.

Seasonal Value   Foliage. Flowers.

Shape   Clumping

Spread   To 2 feet

Height   8 to 12 inches

Soil   Tolerant to soils and to drought, but best with some water. Provide good drainage.

Use   Ground cover. Borders. Containers. Planting strips.

Origin   South Africa

Comments   While this is a clumping Gazania, *G. rigens var. leucolaena* is one that has a trailing habit. The word Gazania may mean riches, referring to the fact that the many different variations provide a wealth of color.

Gazania rigens var. leucolaena

TRAILING GAZANIA

Family Compositae

Leaves Evergreen. An herbaceous perennial. Alternate or fascicled. Entire. Oblanceolate to spatulate. Revolute. Midrib conspicuous, especially on lower side. White tomentose both sides and on the stem. Grayish-white both sides. To about 3 inches long. To 1/2 inch wide. When injured, parts exude a milky substance.

Flowers Yellow. To 2 1/2 inches across. In solitary heads. Regular. Corolla 4 - 5-lobed. Stamens 5. Spring through summer, or most of the year. Opening in the sun.

Fruit An achene. With a pappus.

Environment Full sun. To 20 or 30 degrees.

Pests Aphids. Soil Mealybug. Thrips.

Propagation Seed. Division.

Rate of Growth Rapid

Pruning Keep under control. Cut back as needed. Divide periodically.

Seasonal Value Foliage. Flowers.

Shape Mat-forming and trailing.

Spread Wide

Height 6 to 8 inches

Soil Tolerant to most soils and to drought, but best with some water. Spreading by rhizomes. Aggressive.

Use Ground cover. Hanging baskets. Slopes. Over walls.

Origin South Africa

Comments Formerly named *G. uniflora* or *G. leucolaena*. Cultivars include 'Sunburst', 'Sunglow' and 'Sunrise Yellow'.

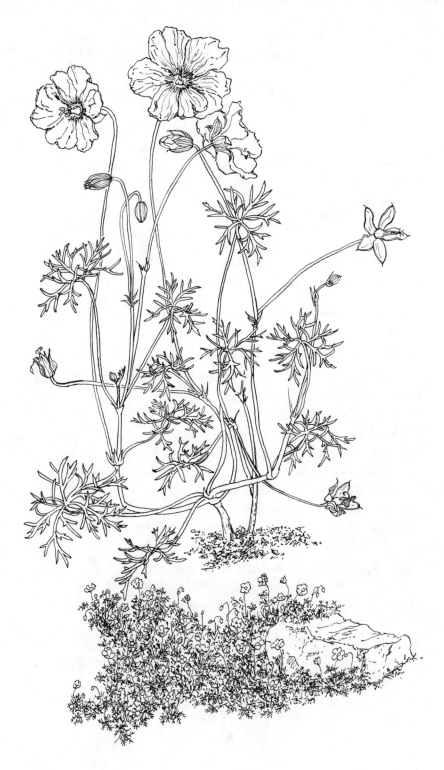

Geranium incanum

Family Geraniaceae

Leaves Mostly evergreen. An herbaceous perennial. Opposite or whorled. Palmately finely dissected. Segments linear. Revolute. Sparsely hairy above. White tomentose below. Medium green. The ultimate segments about 1/4 inch long and 3/16 inch wide.

Flowers Rosy purple to magenta pink. One inch across. Solitary. Regular. Petals 5 and imbricated. Stamens 10. Spring through fall.

Fruit Comprised of stiff carpels, mostly permanently attached to the styles.

Environment Full sun best. Tolerant to partial shade. To 30 or 40 degrees.

Pests Aphids

Propagation Seeds. Cuttings. Self-sows.

Rate of Growth Rapid

Pruning Keep under control. Somewhat aggressive. Spreads by stolons. Head back periodically for best appearance.

Seasonal Value Foliage. Flowers.

Shape Sprawling. Trailing.

Spread 3 to 4 feet or more.

Height 6 to 10 inches

Soil Tolerant. Best with occasional watering. Provide good drainage.

Use Ground cover. Hanging baskets. Over walls. Rock gardens.

Origin South Africa

Comments *Geranium* means crane, referring to the beaklike fruit.

143

Glechoma hederacea

GROUND IVY
GILL-OVER-THE-GROUND

Family Labiatae

Leaves Evergreen. An herbaceous perennial. Opposite. Crenate. Orbicular to reniform. Conspicuously palmately veined. Glandular-dotted and somewhat hairy both sides. Sparsely ciliate. Dull, dark green above. Varying from 1/4 to over one inch across and about as long. Stems squarish or revolute.

Flowers Blue to violet. In axillary verticillasters. Corolla irregular and 2-lipped. Stamens 4. Spring and summer.

Fruit Consisting of 4 glabrous nutlets.

Environment Full sun or partial shade. Tolerant to considerable shade. To below zero.

Pests Aphids. Mites.

Propagation Seed. Cuttings. Division.

Rate of Growth Rapid

Pruning Keep under control. Very invasive. Spreads by rhizomes.

Seasonal Value Foliage. Flowers.

Shape Creeping. Mat-forming.

Spread Wide

Height 3 to 6 inches

Soil Tolerant, but best with periodic watering.

Use Ground cover. Hanging baskets.

Origin Europe

Comments Formerly *Nepeta glechoma* and *N. hederacea*. The word *hederacea* means like Ivy. The plant has hybridized in North America. There is also a variegated form.

Grevillea 'Noell'

NOELL'S GREVILLEA

Family Proteaceae

Leaves Evergreen. Alternate. Entire. Needlelike. Linear. Revolute. Acute. Glabrous both sides. Deeply grooved on lower side. Medium green. To one inch long. About 1/16 inch wide. Stems hairy.

Flowers Pink and white. To 2 inches long. In terminal pairs. In many-flowered racemes. Distinctive. Irregular. Perianth 4-lobed. Stamens 4. Attractive to birds. Spring.

Fruit A coriaceous follicle.

Environment Full sun or partial shade. Does well in coastal areas. To 20 or 30 degrees.

Pests Apparently few.

Propagation Cuttings

Rate of Growth Moderate

Pruning As needed to shape.

Seasonal Value Foliage. Flowers.

Shape Sprawling. Arching.

Spread 4 to 5 feet

Height To 4 feet

Soil Tolerant to soils and to drought. Best, however, with some water. Provide good drainage.

Use Ground cover. Slopes. Over walls.

Origin Australia

Comments Some members of this family are used for dye plants.

Grewia occidentalis

Family   Tiliaceae

Leaves   Evergreen. Alternate. Serrate. 3 to 7-nerved. Lanceolate to rhombic or ovate. Acute or rounded. Either glabrous or pubescent. Dark green. To 3 inches long. About 5/8 inch wide.

Flowers   Lavender. With yellow centers. Axillary. On slender stems. To one inch across. Regular. Petals 5. Stamens numerous. Late spring to fall.

Fruit   A reddish-purple, mostly 4-lobed drupe. To 3/8 inches across.

Environment   Full sun. For temperate areas. Does well on the coast. Tolerant to wind. To 20 or 30 degrees.

Pests   Mealybugs. White Flies. Slugs. Snails.

Propagation   Seed. Cuttings.

Rate of Growth   Rapid

Pruning   After flowering, cut back to encourage more bloom and to control growth.

Seasonal Value   Foliage. Flowers.

Shape   Sprawling, or a semi-vine.

Spread   To 10 feet

Height   6 to 10 feet

Soil   Best when fertile and well-drained. Best with some water. Will respond to Iron sulfate application when chlorotic.

Use   Ground cover. Containers. Espaliers. Hedge. Semi-vine.

Origin   South Africa

Comments   Nurseries often sell this plant under the name of *G. caffra,* however, the latter has yellow flowers.

Gypsophila paniculata 'Pink Fairy'

BABY'S BREATH

Family   Caryophyllaceae

Leaves   Evergreen. An herbaceous perennial. Opposite to fascicled or whorled. Entire. Linear to lanceolate. Midrib conspicuous, especially below. Glaucous and glandular-dotted both sides. Mature leaves mostly glabrous. Ciliate. Grayish. Leaves vary in size, those below being larger. Length from 1/2 to 1 1/2 inches. Width from 1/8 to 1/4 inch. Stems glaucous.

Flowers   Pinkish (White with the species). Each about 1/4 inch across. In loose, open, many-flowered panicles. Profuse. Regular. Petals 5. Stamens usually 10. July-October.

Fruit   A 4-valved capsule.

Environment   Full sun. To below zero.

Pests   Aphids. Slugs. Snails.

Propagation   Seed. Cuttings. Division.

Rate of Growth   Rapid

Pruning   Cut back after flowering to encourage new growth and to eliminate fruiting and seeding.

Seasonal Value   Foliage. Flowers.

Shape   Sprawling

Spread   To 3 feet or more.

Height   To 18 inches

Soil   Alkaline and with sufficent water.

Use   Ground cover. Cut flowers. Rock gardens. Over walls. Hanging baskets.

Origin   Asia. Europe.

Comments   *Gypsophila* means Gypsum-loving. Refers to the preference for soils with Calcium in them. Gypsum is Calcium sulfate. The plant is used by the floral trade. In the landscape it provides an airy, delicate effect. Cultivars besides this one include 'Alba', 'Compacta', 'Flore Pleno' and 'Grandiflora'.

Hedera canariensis

ALGERIAN IVY

Family Araliaceae

Leaves Evergreen. Alternate. Entire. Juvenile ones ovate and entire or 3 to 7-lobed. Cordate. Glabrous. Light to medium green. To 6 inches across and about as long. Veining conspicuous. Adult leaves are ovate to lanceolate and are usually darker. They are also glabrous. Stress and cold will cause leaf bronzing.

Flowers Small. Greenish. In panicled umbels. Only on the adult branches. Regular. Petals 5. Stamens 5. Fall.

Fruit A black berry.

Environment Full sun or partial shade. Tolerant to considerable shade. Provide shade where hot. To about 20 degrees.

Pests Aphids. Caterpillars. Greedy and Nigra Scales. Mites. Slugs. Snails. Bacterial Leaf Spot.

Propagation Cuttings. Division.

Rate of Growth Slow to start, then rapid.

Pruning Keep under control. Invasive. Cut to ground level periodically to encourage new growth and to remove injured leaves.

Seasonal Value Foliage

Shape Spreading. Trailing. Climbing.

Spread Wide

Height To 18 inches or to 75 feet as a vine.

Soil Tolerant, but best if fertile and with sufficient moisture. Provide good drainage.

Use Ground cover. Erosion control. Slopes. Over a wall or a fence. Vine.

Origin Canary Islands. North Africa.

Comments Formerly *H. algeriensis* and *H. maderensis*. This plant is more tolerant than is *Hedera helix*. It is commonly planted on the freeways of California. There are cultivars such as 'Variegata'.

Hedera helix

Family   Araliaceae

Leaves   Evergreen. Alternate. Juvenile leaves variable, but usually 3 to 5-lobed. Mostly entire. Triangular to ovate in outline. Adult leaves elliptic to ovate and not lobed. Entire. Dark green and glabrous above, with conspicuous lighter veining. Stellate hairs on petiole and lower side. Varying from 1/2 inch to about 5 inches across and as long.

Flowers   Greenish. In umbels arranged in panicles. Regular. Petals 5. Stamens 5. In the fall.

Fruit   A black berry. Globose. 1/4 inch across.

Environment   Best in some shade where hot, otherwise may burn. Tolerant to wind, considerable shade. To zero degrees.

Pests   Many, to include these: Greedy, Ivy and Nigra Scales. Mealybug. Cyclamen and other Mites. Bacterial Leaf Spot. Fungus Leaf Spot. Slugs. Snails.

Propagation   Cuttings. Division. Layering.

Rate of Growth   Moderate to rapid. Slow to start.

Pruning   Keep under control. Very invasive. Spreads by rhizomes and stolons. Cut to ground periodically. Keep off of trees.

Seasonal Value   Foliage

Shape   Spreading. Trailing. Climbing.

Spread   Wide

Height   One foot, or to 90 feet.

Soil   Best if fertile and well-drained. Drought-tolerant, but best with some water.

Use   Ground cover. Containers. Erosion control. Hanging baskets. Indoors. Slopes. Over walls.

Origin   Asia. Europe.

Comments   Will naturalize. When growing as a vine will cling by holdfasts which are along the stems. Mature stems produce the flowers and fruit and these stems will grow as shrubs rather than as vines. There are numerous cultivars. The stems may be several inches thick when older.

154

155

Hedera helix 'Hahn's Self-Branching'

Family Araliaceae

Leaves Evergreen. Alternate. Mostly entire. Palmately 3 to 5-lobed. Lobes acute. Ovate. Veins conspicuous and lighter-colored on upper side. Mature growth mostly glabrous both sides. On the young foliage are seen stellate hairs on both sides. Leaves glandular-dotted both sides. Light green. 2 to 3 inches long and about 1½ inches wide. Stems mostly glabrous, pinkish.

Flowers Greenish. In umbels arranged in panicles. Regular. Petals 5. Stamens 5. Fall.

Fruit A globose, black berry.

Environment Full sun or partial shade. Often best in some shade. Tolerant to considerable shade. To zero degrees.

Pests Mostly the same ones that attack the parent plant, H. helix.

Propagation Cuttings

Rate of Growth Rapid, once established.

Pruning Keep under control. Very invasive. Spreading by stolons and by rhizomes.

Seasonal Value Foliage.

Shape Creeping. Climbing.

Spread Wide

Height 8 to 12 inches. More as a vine.

Soil Tolerant to soils and to drought, but best with some water.

Use Ground cover. Containers. Erosion Control. Hanging baskets. Indoors. Slopes. As a vine.

Origin The parent plant is from Asia and Europe.

Comments The leaves are a lighter green and the lobes are more acute and there are more small terminal leaves than with *H. helix*. This is a very clean-appearing plant in the landscape.

157

Hedyotis caerulea

Family Rubiaceae

Leaves Evergreen. Deciduous where cold. An herbaceous perennial. Opposite. Entire. Obovate to spatulate. Glabrous and glandular-dotted both sides. Light to medium green. About 1/4 inch long. To 1/8 inch wide. Stems squarish, glabrous and glandular-dotted.

Flowers Light lavender, blue or white. With a yellow eye that appears as an 8-lobed cross. To 1/2 inch across. Salverform. Usually solitary. Regular. Petals 4. Stamens 4. Spring-summer.

Fruit A capsule which is about 1/8 inch across.

Environment Full sun to partial shade. Perhaps best in some shade. To below zero.

Pests Aphids. Mites.

Propagation Seed. Cuttings. Division.

Rate of Growth Rapid

Pruning Keep under control. Spreads by stolons.

Seasonal Value Foliage. Flowers.

Shape Mat-forming. Tufted.

Spread Wide

Height To 6 or 7 inches

Soil Fertile. Moist. Well-drained.

Use Ground cover. Rock gardens.

Origin Nova Scotia to Quebec and Wisconsin, south to Georgia and Arkansas.

Comments Formerly *Houstonia caerulea*. *caerulea* means dark blue.

Helianthemum nummularium 'Rose'

Family Cistaceae

Leaves Evergreen. An herbaceous perennial. Mostly opposite. Entire. Oblong to lanceolate. Revolute. 2-ranked. Hairy both sides. Grayish. 1 to 2 inches long. About 1/4 inch wide. Stems white-hairy.

Flowers Pink or dusty rose, fading to an apricot color. To one inch across. In many-flowered loose racemes. Each flower lasting only one day, but others keep opening. Regular. Petals 5. Stamens numerous. Spring and summer.

Fruit An ovoid, 3-valved capsule.

Environment Full sun. Tolerant to seacoast conditions. To below zero.

Pests Aphids. Fungus Leaf Spot.

Propagation Cuttings. Division.

Rate of Growth Slow to moderate.

Pruning Cut back after flowering in order to encourage more bloom.

Seasonal Value Foliage. Flowers.

Shape Mat-forming

Spread To 3 feet

Height 8 to 12 inches or more.

Soil Tolerant to soils, including those alkaline, and to drought. Provide good drainage. Cultivation not recommended.

Use Ground cover. Containers. Rock gardens. Slopes. Over walls. Hanging baskets.

Origin Europe

Comments *Helianthemum* means Sunflower. Former names of the parent plant include *H. chamaecistus* and *Cistus nummularium*. The plant is said to be fire-resistant.

Herniaria glabra

GREEN CARPET
RUPTUREWORT

Family Caryophyllaceae

Leaves Evergreen. An herbaceous perennial. Opposite. Entire. Ovate to elliptic. Sometimes cuspidate. Glabrous and glandular-dotted both sides. Ciliate. Bright green, turning reddish with cold weather. From 1/8 to 3/8 inch long. About 1/8 inch wide. Stems hairy and glandular-dotted.

Flowers White. 1/4 inch long. Crowded in axillary clusters. Regular. Petals zero. Stamens 5.

Fruit An indehiscent nutlet, with one seed.

Environment Full sun or partial shade. To below zero.

Pests Aphids

Propagation Seed. Division.

Rate of Growth Rapid

Pruning Keep under control. Spreads by stolons. Usually not too aggressive.

Seasonal Value Foliage. Fall coloring (Leaves).

Shape Mat-forming

Spread Wide

Height 2 to 3 inches

Soil Tolerant, but needs moisture and good drainage.

Use Ground cover. Between stepping stones. Parking strips.

Origin Africa. Asia. Europe. Turkey.

Comments The name *Herniaria* refers to the alleged properties for healing of hernias or ruptures.

Heterocentron elegans

SPANISH-SHAWL

Family Melastomataceae

Leaves Evergreen. An herbaceous perennial. Opposite. Entire to mostly crenate. Ovate to oblong. Glabrous or somewhat strigose, especially on the veins. Glandular-dotted both sides. Sparsely ciliate. Green surface blotched with red. 3-veined from base. Length 1/2 to one inch. Width 1/4 to 1/2 inch. Stems squarish, reddish, hairy.

Flowers Purplish-red (Magenta). To one inch or more across. Solitary and terminal on laterals. Regular. Petals 4. Stamens 8. May-August.

Fruit A 4-valved capsule.

Environment Partial shade best. Tolerant to considerable shade. To 30 or 35 degrees.

Pests Aphids. Mites. Slugs. Snails.

Propagation Cuttings. Division.

Rate of Growth Moderate to slow

Pruning Keep under control. Spreads by stolons.

Seasonal Value Foliage. Flowers.

Shape Compact. Mat-forming. Trailing or vinelike.

Spread Wide

Height To 6 inches

Soil Tolerant to soils and to drought, but best if fertile and with sufficient water.

Use Ground cover. Containers. Hanging baskets. Rock gardens.

Origin Guatemala. Honduras. Mexico.

Comments Formerly named *Schizocentron elegans* and *Heeria elegans*. *Heterocentron* means with split spurs, referring to the anthers.

164

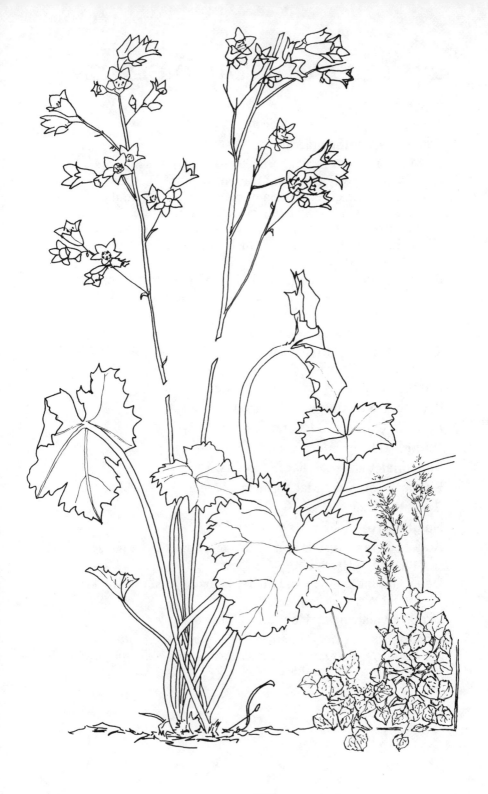

165

Heuchera sanguinea

Family Saxifragaceae

Leaves Evergreen. An herbaceous perennial. Leaves basal and in tufts. Crenate. Orbicular to cordate or ovate. Conspicuously palmately veined. Palmately 5 to 9-lobed. Glandular-dotted both sides and pubescent both sides only on the veins. Ciliate. Dark green. Reddish in the winter. One to 2 inches across and about as long. Petioles hairy and to 5 inches long.

Flowers Bright red or pink. Campanulate. To 1/2 inch long and 1/4 inch across. In cymose panicles. Stems to 20 inches or more long. Regular. Petals 5. Stamens 5. Attractive to Hummingbirds. April-September.

Fruit A capsule about 1/2 inch across.

Environment Full sun or partial shade. Shade where warm. To zero degrees.

Pests Soil Mealybug. Root Knot Nematode. Slugs. Snails. Mildew.

Propagation Cuttings. Division.

Rate of Growth Moderate to rapid

Pruning Remove dead flowers. Divide periodically.

Seasonal Value Foliage. Flowers.

Shape Mounding

Spread To 12 inches

Height To 12 inches

Soil Best if fertile and on the moist side. Provide good drainage.

Use Ground cover. Borders. Containers. Cut flowers. Rock gardens.

Origin Arizona and New Mexico to Mexico

Comments *sanguinea* means blood-red. Flower colors vary from red or pink to white, depending upon the cultivar. Cultivars include 'Alba', 'Fire Sprite', 'Freedom', 'Grandiflora', 'June Bride', 'Maxima', 'Oxfordii', 'Splendens' and 'Virginalis'.

Hosta sieboldiana

Family Liliaceae

Leaves Deciduous. An herbaceous perennial. Basal. Entire. Ovate to elliptic. Mostly acuminate. Conspicuously veined, with about 24 parallel veins. Glandular-dotted and glabrous both sides. Glaucous below. Dark green or grayish above. From 10 to 15 inches long and 5 to 6 inches wide. Petioles glandular-dotted and glabrous.

Flowers Pale lavender. 1 1/2 inches long. On a 6 to 10-flowered raceme. Scapose, with the scape usually shorter than the leaves. Flowers are funnelform and 6-lobed. Racemes are one-sided. Regular. Stamens 6. Spring and summer.

Fruit A 3-valved capsule.

Environment Full sun or partial shade. Usually best in some shade. Tolerant to considerable shade. Probably more gray in sun. Does well in cold areas. Tolerant to below zero.

Pests Slugs and Snails.

Propagation Seed. Division.

Rate of Growth Rapid

Pruning Usually little needed. Spreads by short rhizomes.

Seasonal Value Foliage. Flowers. Grown, however, primarily for the foliage, though the flowers are attractive.

Shape Clumping, with overlapping leaves.

Spread 2 to 3 feet

Height One foot or more.

Soil Best if fertile, moist. Responds to fertilizing, but the foliage may be better if plant is not fertilized.

Use Ground cover. Borders. Containers. For shaded areas. Flowers and foliage effective in indoor arrangements.

Origin Japan

Comments Formerly *H. glauca, Funkia glauca, Hemerocallis sieboldiana, Funkia sieboldiana* and *Niobe sieboldiana.* There are many species and cultivars.

Hypericum calycinum

Family Hypericaceae

Leaves Evergreen or semi-evergreen. Opposite or whorled. New growth especially, 4-ranked. Entire. Ovate to oblong. Glabrous and glandular-dotted both sides. Glaucous and conspicuously net-veined below. Mature growth is dark green. Cold weather causes discloration. To 4 inches long. To one inch in width. Stems glabrous and somewhat angular. Becoming woody near base.

Flowers Bright yellow. To 3 inches across. Solitary or in terminal cymes. Regular. Petals 5. Stamens numerous and in 5 clusters. Spring through summer.

Fruit An ovoid capsule. To 4 inches long. July-September.

Environment Full sun or partial shade. Best in some shade where hot. To zero degrees.

Pests Aphids. Greedy Scale. Klamath Beetle. Thrips. Mildew. Rust.

Propagation Seed. Cuttings.

Rate of Growth Rapid

Pruning Keep under control. Very aggressive. Spreads by rhizomes and stolons. Cut to ground at least every other year. Comes back looking much better. Do this after frost danger is over.

Seasonal Value Foliage. Flowers.

Shape Upright. Compact.

Spread Wide

Height 12-18 inches

Soil Tolerant to soils and to drought. Best, however, with some water.

Use Ground cover. Erosion control. Slopes.

Origin Asia Minor. Europe.

Comments Was once *H. grandiflorum*. The Klamath Beetle was introduced years ago to help control Klamath Weed, *Hypericum perforatum*. Recently this insect has been attacking *Hypericum calycinum*.

170

Hypericum coris

Family Hypericaceae

Leaves Evergreen. An herbaceous perennial. Entire. Opposite or in whorls of 3 or sometimes 4. New shoots 4-ranked. Linear. Glabrous and glandular-dotted both sides. Grayish. 1/2 to one inch long.

Flowers Yellow. One inch or more across. In few-flowered, loose cymes. Regular. Petals 5. Stamens numerous and in 3 groups. Spring-early summer.

Fruit A capsule.

Environment Full sun. To about 30 or 35 degrees.

Pests Aphids. Thrips.

Propagation Seed. Cuttings.

Rate of Growth Rapid

Pruning Keep under control. Spreads by rhizomes.

Seasonal Value Foliage. Flowers.

Shape Mat-forming

Spread Wide

Height 6 to 12 inches or more.

Soil Tolerant if well-drained.

Use Ground cover. Containers. Rock gardens.

Origin Europe

Comments Much used in the southern part of the United States.

Iberis sempervirens

EVERGREEN CANDYTUFT
CANDYTUFT

Family Cruciferae

Leaves Evergreen. An herbaceous perennial. Alternate. Entire. Linear to oblanceolate. Glabrous and glandular-dotted both sides and on stems. Dark glossy green. One to 1 1/2 inches long. About 1/8 to 1/4 inch in width. Stems are stiff, almost woody, and they are somewhat reddish.

Flowers White. In umbels which are one to 2 inches across. Regular. Petals 4. Stamens 6. Spring through summer.

Fruit A broad, nearly orbicular silique which is 2-valved.

Environment Full sun to partial shade. To below zero.

Pests Aphids. Mites. Soil Mealybug. Mildew.

Propagation Seed. Cuttings. Division. Self-layering.

Rate of Growth Rapid

Pruning Remove dead flowers.

Seasonal Value Foliage. Flowers.

Shape Roundish and sprawling.

Spread To 18 inches

Height To 18 inches

Soil Tolerant. Does well in somewhat alkaline soils. Best with some water.

Use Ground cover. Containers. Cut flowers. Rock gardens.

Origin Europe

Comments Was once *I. garrexiana*. The word *Iberis* is one relating to Spain, where some species are native. The word *sempervirens* means evergreen. This plant does not transplant easily. The cultivars include 'Compacta', 'Little Gem', 'Nana', 'Purity', 'Snowflake' and 'Superba'.

Justicia brandegeana

Family Acanthaceae

Leaves Evergreen. Opposite. Entire. Lanceolate to ovate. Glabrous and glandular-dotted both sides except hairy on veins below. Ciliate. Yellowish-green. To 3 inches long and to one inch wide. Stems squarish, glandular-dotted and hairy.

Flowers White, with reddish spots on the lower lip. In terminal, pendulous spikes which are to 6 inches long or more. The conspicuous bracts are bronze to yellow-green. They overlap the flowers. Irregular. Corolla 2-lipped. Stamens 2. Summer, or much longer.

Fruit A 2-celled capsule.

Environment Full sun or partial shade. Usually best in some shade. To about 30 degrees.

Pests Aphids

Propagation Seed. Cuttings.

Rate of Growth Rapid

Pruning Cut back lightly to keep compact.

Seasonal Value Foliage. Flowers. Bracts.

Shape Erect

Spread 3 to 4 feet

Height To 3 feet

Soil Fertile, with some moisture. Should not be too dry nor too wet.

Use Ground cover. Containers.

Origin Mexico

Comments Formerly *Beloperone guttata* and *Drejerella guttata*. *Beloperone lutea* is probably *J. brandegeana*. Cultivars include 'Chartreusse' and 'Yellow Queen'. Shrimp Plant has been naturalized in Florida. *J. californica* is native to California.

Lampranthus spectabilis

Family   Aizoaceae

Leaves   Evergreen. An herbaceous perennial. Opposite. Entire. Cylindrical to 3-angled. Somewhat curved. Succulent. With reddish tips. Mostly glabrous. Grayish. 2 to 3 inches long. To 1/4 inch wide. Stems squarish, hairy and glandular-dotted.

Flowers   Petals a brilliant purple. 2 to 3 inches across. On stems which are 3 to 6 inches long. Regular. Solitary or in threes. Stamens numerous. Spring.

Fruit   A 5-valved capsule.

Environment   Full sun. To about 20 degrees.

Pests   Aphids. Mealybug.

Propagation   Seed. Cuttings.

Rate of Growth   Rapid

Pruning   Keep under control. Replant regularly for best appearance.

Seasonal Value   Foliage. Flowers.

Shape   Trailing. Creeping. Prostrate.

Spread   Wide

Height   6 to 12 inches

Soil   Tolerant to soils and to drought, but best with some water during dry periods.

Use   Ground cover. Erosion control. Hanging baskets. Indoor planters. Rock gardens. Slopes.

Origin   South Africa

Comments   Formerly *Mesembryanthemum spectabilis*. *Lampranthus* means glossy flower.

Lantana montevidensis

Family Verbenaceae

Leaves Evergreen, or nearly so. Opposite or whorled. Ciliate. Coarsely crenate. Ovate. Glabrous above, hairy below. Revolute. Rugose. Dark green, turning darker with cold. Pungent, 1/2 to one inch long. To 1/2 inch wide. Stems weak and hairy.

Flowers Rose pink to lilac. About 1/4 inch across. In compact, terminal heads which are to one inch across. Irregular. Corolla 4-lobed. Stamens 4. Most of the year.

Fruit A cluster of small, purple drupes. Seldom seen.

Environment Full sun. Tolerant to wind, to 26 degrees. Will usually recover from cold injury. Susceptible to Mildew in shade.

Pests Mealybug. White Fly. Mites. Nematodes. Mildew.

Propagation Cuttings. Self-layering.

Rate of Growth Moderate

Pruning Keep under control. Head back after danger of frost.

Seasonal Value Foliage. Flowers.

Shape Sprawling. Trailing.

Spread To 4 feet or more.

Height 2 to 3 feet

Soil Tolerant to soils and to drought, but best with some water.

Use Ground cover. Erosion control. Hanging baskets. Slopes. Over walls.

Origin South America

Comments Formerly *L. sellowiana* and *L. delicatissima,* and also *Lippia delicata* and *Lippia montevidensis.* Is crossed with *L. camara* to produce cultivars. The plant has naturalized from Florida to Texas and in the Hawaiian Islands. The fruit may be poisonous.

180

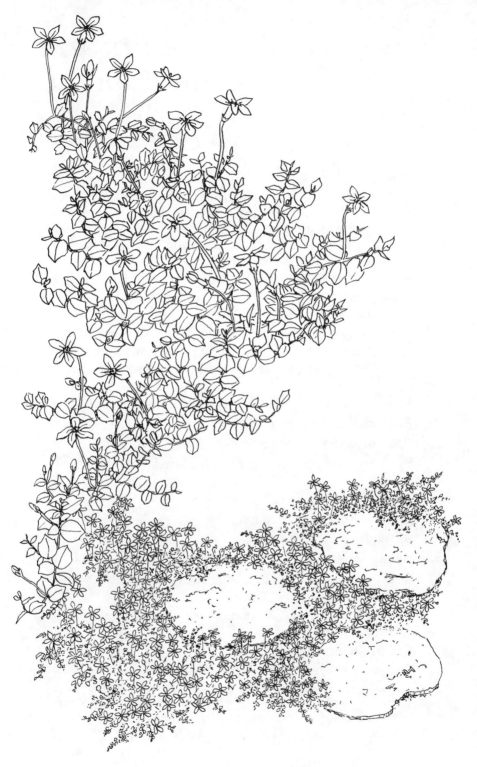

181

Laurentia fluviatilis

Family Lobeliaceae

Leaves Evergreen. An herbaceous perennial. Alternate. Entire and somewhat lobed. Ovate to orbicular. Glandular-dotted and slightly pubescent both sides. Purplish below. Ciliate. A medium, dull green. 1/4 inch long and about as wide. Stems weak and hairy.

Flowers Pale blue to purplish. Pale outside. To 3/8 inch or more across. Solitary or in racemes. Stellate. Irregular. Corolla 5-lobed. Stamens 5. Spring and summer, and at other times.

Fruit A capsule.

Environment Full sun or partial shade. The latter is usually best. To 25 degrees.

Pests Aphids

Propagation Seed. Cuttings. Division.

Rate of Growth Moderate to rapid

Pruning Remove the dead flowers.

Seasonal Value Foliage. Flowers.

Shape Mat-forming

Spread 6 to 12 inches or more.

Height 2 to 3 inches

Soil Fertile, moist and well-drained.

Use Ground cover. Between stepping stones. Rock gardens.

Origin Australia. Tasmania. New Zealand.

Comments Formerly *Isotoma fluviatilis.* Is somewhat tolerant to foot traffic.

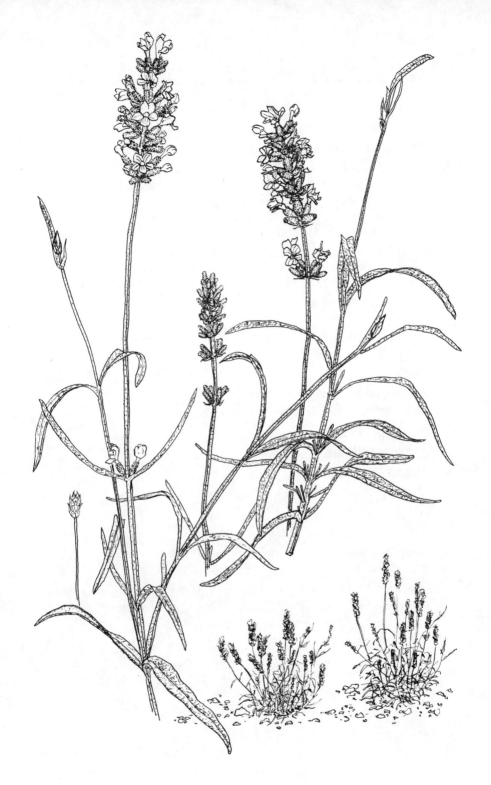

183

Lavandula angustifolia 'Hidcote'

ENGLISH LAVENDER

Family Labiatae

Leaves Evergreen. Opposite. Entire. Linear to lanceolate to oblanceolate. Revolute. Pubescent both sides, with stellate hairs. Conspicuous midrib below. Glandular-dotted both sides. Grayish. Aromatic. One to 2 inches long. To 1/4 inch wide. Stems hairy, glossy brown and squarish.

Flowers Deep lavender. In verticillasters which are 6 to 10 flowered and to 3 inches long. Fragrant. Irregular. Corolla 5-lobed. Stamens 4. July-August.

Fruit Consisting of 4 glabrous nutlets.

Environment Full sun. From zero to 10 degrees.

Pests Aphids. Mites.

Propagation Seed. Cuttings. Division.

Rate of Growth Moderate to slow

Pruning Remove dead flowers.

Seasonal Value Foliage. Flowers. Fragrance (Foliage, flowers).

Shape Compact. Erect.

Spread 18 inches

Height To 18 inches

Soil Tolerant to soils and to drought. Good drainage important.

Use Ground cover. Borders. Herb gardens. Rock gardens.

Origin Mediterranean

Comments The parent plant was once *L. officinalis*, *L. spica* and *L. vera*. *Lávandula* means to wash, referring to the use of Lavender in the bath. It is also used in perfumery and for other toiletries and for its medicinal properties. Cultivars besides this one include 'Alba', 'Atropurpurea', 'Compacta', 'Dutch', 'Fragrance', 'Munstead', 'Nana', 'Rosea', 'Twickel Purple' and Waltham'.

Liriope muscari
BIG BLUE LILYTURF

Family Liliaceae

Leaves Evergreen. An herbaceous perennial. Basal. Entire. Linear. Straplike. Somewhat revolute. Parallel veining which is prominent, as is the midrib below. Glabrous and glandular-dotted both sides. Ciliate. Dark green. To 2 feet in length. To 3/4 inch wide.

Flowers Dark purple. Each about 1/4 inch across. In dense racemes which are 6 to 8 inches long and on stems which are 12 inches or longer. Protruding above the leaves in young plants and partly hidden when plants are older. Regular. Petals 6. Stamens 6. Profuse. July-August or longer.

Fruit A shiny, black, fleshy capsule. Globose. About 1/3 inch across. With one or 2 seeds.

Environment Partial shade usually best. Tolerant to considerable shade and in cooler areas can take full sun. To zero degrees or lower.

Pests Soil Mealybug. Slugs. Snails.

Propagation Division

Rate of Growth Moderate to rapid

Pruning Cut back in spring to remove undesirable foliage and to encourage new growth. Root system matted, descending, with a few thick tubers.

Seasonal Value Foliage. Flowers.

Shape Mounding

Spread 12 to 18 inches

Height 12 to 18 inches

Soil Best in a fertile soil, with sufficient moisture. Provide good drainage.

Use Ground cover. Borders. Containers. Indoors. Around pools. Rock gardens.

Origin China and Japan

Comments There are many cultivars, including one with variegated foliage. *L. muscari* is said to be the tallest of the Liriopes. It differs from *L. spicata* in that the plant is larger, the leaves are wider, darker and stiffer. Also, the root system is tuberous, descending and without rhizomes.

Lithodora diffusa

Family Boraginaceae

Leaves Evergreen. Alternate. Entire. Linear to lanceolate. Revolute. Midrib conspicuous, especially below. Pubescent and glandular-dotted both sides. Grayish. 1/4 to one inch long. To 1/4 inch wide. Young stems hairy. Older ones glabrous and woody.

Flowers A brilliant blue. Striped with reddish-violet. Tubular. In few-flowered cymes. Each flower 1/2 inch across. Regular. Corolla 5-lobed. Stamens 5. Spring-summer.

Fruit Consists of 4 striated nutlets.

Environment Full sun or partial shade. Some shade where warm. To about 20 degrees.

Pests Aphids

Propagation Seed. Cuttings. Layering.

Rate of Growth Moderate

Pruning Keep under control.

Seasonal Value Foliage. Flowers.

Shape Prostrate to mounding.

Spread 2 feet or more

Height 6 to 12 inches

Soil Acid. Fertile. Moist. Well-drained.

Use Ground cover. Hanging baskets. Rock gardens. Over walls.

Origin Europe. Morocco.

Comments Formerly *Lithospermum diffusum* and *L. prostratum*. *Lithospermum* means stone seed, referring to the stonelike seed. *diffusa* means spreading. The cultivars include 'Grace Ward' and 'Heavenly Blue'.

188

Loropetalum chinense

Family Hamameliadaceae

Leaves Evergreen. Alternate. Entire. Ovate to elliptic. Revolute. Stellate-pubescent both sides, especially along the veins. Prominently net-veined. Ciliate. Scabrous. Oblique at the base. Some leaves turn yellow to red during the year. To 2 inches long and to one inch wide. Stems pubescent and somewhat reddish.

Flowers Whitish. About 3/4 inch across. In terminal clusters of 4 to 8. Regular. Petals 4. Stamens 4. Petals are twisted. Spring.

Fruit A woody capsule.

Environment Full sun where cool. Partial shade where warm. To below zero.

Pests Aphids. Thrips.

Propagation Seed. Cuttings. Grafting.

Rate of Growth Moderate to slow

Pruning As needed.

Seasonal Value Foliage. Flowers.

Shape Compact, with arching branches. Somewhat tiered.

Spread 3 to 5 feet

Height Usually 3 to 5 feet. Older plants could go to 10 feet.

Soil Best when fertile, moist and well-drained.

Use Ground cover. Containers. Hanging baskets. Woodland areas.

Origin China. Japan.

Comments Was once named *Hamamelis chinensis*.

Lotus berthelotii

Family Leguminosae

Leaves Evergreen. An herbaceous perennial. Alternate. Odd-pinnately compound (appearing whorled or fascicled). With 3 to 7 leaflets. Entire. Linear. Needlelike. Pubescent. Grayish. Each to 1/2 inch long and 1/16 inch wide. Stems pubescent. Older stems somewhat woody, to 2 feet long.

Flowers Scarlet. To one inch long. Shaped as a parrot's beak. Profuse. Several together. Axillary. Irregular. Corolla 5-lobed. Stamens 10. June and July.

Fruit A narrow, 2-valved legume.

Environment Full sun to partial shade. May die back if too cold. To about 30 degrees.

Pests Black Scale. Mealybug.

Propagation Seed. Cuttings. Division.

Rate of Growth Rapid

Pruning Remove dead flowers. Cut back to control.

Seasonal Value Foliage. Flowers.

Shape Trailing

Spread 2 to 3 feet

Height 3 to 4 inches

Soil Tolerant. Best with some water. Too much, however, will cause decline or death.

Use Ground cover. Hanging baskets. Slopes. Over walls.

Origin Cape Verde and Canary Islands

Comments Presenting a good contrast between the gray foliage and the bright red flowers.

Lysimachia nummularia

Family   Primulaceae

Leaves   Evergreen. An herbaceous perennial. Opposite or whorled. Entire. Nearly orbicular. Glabrous and often glandular-dotted both sides. Bright green. 1/2 to one inch long and about as wide. Stems long, trailing glabrous and somewhat angular.

Flowers   Yellow, with dark dots. To one inch across. Solitary and axillary. Regular. Corolla 5-lobed. Stamens usually 5. Summer until fall.

Fruit   A 5-valved capsule.

Environment   Partial shade best. To below zero.

Pests   Aphids. Mites.

Propagation   Seed. Division. Self-rooting at every part.

Rate of Growth   Rapid

Pruning   Keep under control. Spreading by stolons. Can be mowed. Very invasive.

Seasonal Value   Foliage. Flowers.

Shape   A low, creeping mat.

Spread   Wide

Height   2 to 6 inches

Soil   Tolerant, but moisture necessary.

Use   Ground cover. Hanging baskets. Over walls.

Origin   Europe

Comments   The word *nummularia* refers to the coin-shaped leaves. This plant has naturalized over North America. It can be and sometimes is considered to be a weed. It is sometimes used as an aquarium plant, where it grows in water. The cultivar 'Aurea' has yellow leaves.

Mentha requienii

Family Labiatae

Leaves Evergreen. An herbaceous perennial. Opposite. Entire. Ovate to cordate to nearly orbicular. Glandular-dotted both sides. Most leaves appear to be glabrous. A few are sparsely hairy. Dark green and strongly aromatic. About 1/8 inch across. About as long, or somewhat longer. Stems weak and pubescent.

Flowers Light purple. Tiny. In loose, few-flowered whorls. Irregular. Corolla limb 4-lobed. Stamens 4. Summer.

Fruit Comprised of 4 nutlets.

Environment Full sun or partial shade. Perhaps best in the latter. To nearly zero degrees. May die down, but usually recovers, or at least seed germinates.

Pests Aphids. Slugs. Snails.

Propagation Seed. Division.

Rate of Growth Rapid

Pruning Keep under control. Spreads by rhizomes. Invasive.

Seasonal Value Foliage. Flowers. Fragrance (Leaves).

Shape Mat-forming

Spread Wide

Height 1/2 to 2 inches

Soil Fertile, moist and well-drained.

Use Ground cover. Containers. Between stepping stones. Herb gardens.

Origin Corsica. Sardinia.

Comments Was once *Menthella requienii*. The generic name is from the name of a nymph whose name was Minte. Has naturalized in Western Europe. For best appearance, replace periodically.

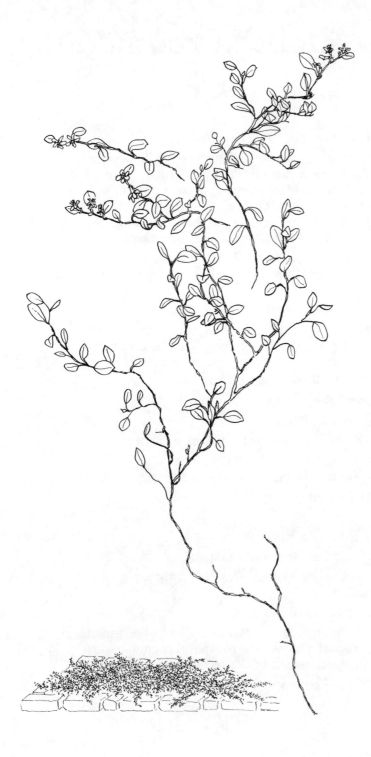

197

Muehlenbeckia axillaris

Family Polygonaceae

Leaves Evergreen. An herbaceous perennial. Alternate. Entire. Oblong to nearly orbicular. Margins reddish. Glabrous both sides. Dark to bronzy green. To 1/4 inch long and nearly as wide. Stems wiry, reddish and glandular-dotted.

Flowers Yellow-green. About 3/16 inch across. Solitary or in twos. Axillary. Dioecious or polygamous. Regular. Petals 5. Stamens 8. Anthers red to pink.

Fruit Usually white. An ovoid, 3-angled achene. Enclosed in a fleshy calyx, resembling a berry.

Environment Full sun or partial shade. To 20 or 30 degrees.

Pests Aphids

Propagation Division

Rate of Growth Moderate

Pruning Keep under control. Spreads by rhizomes.

Seasonal Value Foliage

Shape Sprawling, clumping, matting.

Spread Wide

Height 2 to 4 inches

Soil Tolerant, but needing water in the summer, along with good drainage.

Use Ground cover. Rock gardens.

Origin New Zealand

Comments Formerly *Polygonum axillaris* and *Calacinum axillare*. The word *axillaris* refers to the axillary flowers.

Myoporum parvifolium

Family Myoporaceae

Leaves Evergreen. An herbaceous perennial. Alternate. Irregularly toothed to nearly entire. Oblanceolate. Glabrous, warty and glandular-dotted both sides. Bright green. 1/2 to one inch long. To 1/4 inch wide. Stems glabrous, warty and glandular-dotted.

Flowers White. Axillary. Campanulate. 3/8 inch across. Solitary or in axillary clusters. Usually regular. Corolla usually 5-lobed. Stamens 4. Summer.

Fruit A purplish, somewhat succulent drupe. Less than 1/8 inch across.

Environment Full sun or partial shade. Does well along the coast. Tolerant to salt spray, seaside conditions. To about 25 degrees.

Pests Aphids

Propagation Seed. Cuttings. Layering.

Rate of Growth Rapid

Pruning Keep under control. Spreads by stolons.

Seasonal Value Foliage. Flowers.

Shape A spreading, trailing mat.

Spread 5 feet or more.

Height 3 to 6 inches or more.

Soil Tolerant. Best on the dry side, with only periodic irrigation. Needs good drainage. Somewhat drought-tolerant.

Use Ground cover. Erosion control. Hanging baskets. Slopes. Over walls.

Origin Australia

Comments *Myoporum* refers to the glandular-dotted leaves. The plant is said to be fire-resistant. It is not tolerant to traffic.

201

Nierembergia hippomanica var. violacea

CUP FLOWER
DWARF CUP FLOWER

Family Solanaceae

Leaves Evergreen. An herbaceous perennial. Alternate. Entire. Linear to lanceolate. Pubescent both sides. Medium green. To one inch long. 1/8 inch wide or more. Stems hairy.

Flowers Blue to violet. To one inch across. Cup-shaped. Solitary on tips of new growth. Regular. Corolla 5-lobed. Stamens 4. All summer.

Fruit A 2-valved capsule.

Environment Full sun. To 20 or 30 degrees.

Pests Aphids

Propagation Seed. Cuttings.

Rate of Growth Rapid

Pruning Cut back to stimulate new growth.

Seasonal Value Foliage. Flowers.

Shape Upright, sprawling.

Spread 12 to 15 inches

Height 12 to 15 inches

Soil Best when fertile and with sufficient moisture. Fairly drought-tolerant.

Use Ground cover. Bedding plant. Borders. Containers.

Origin Argentina

Comments This plant has naturalized in some areas. 'Purple Robe' is a cultivar.

Ophiopogon japonicus

MONDO GRASS

Family Liliaceae

Leaves Evergreen. An herbaceous perennial. Basal.
Linear to oblong-lanceolate, and narrowing into the
petiole. Grasslike. Serrate, almost bristly. Glabrous but
scabrous. Arching. With 5 to 7 prominent, parallel veins.
Dark green. To 12 inches or more in length. About 1/8
inch wide.

Flowers Light lavender. Each about 1/4 inch across. In
short, loose, few-flowered, terminal, pendulous racemes.
Hidden by the foliage. Regular. Peraianth 6-lobed.
Stamens 6. Early summer.

Fruit A blue, globose capsule. About 1/4 inch across. In
tight clusters.

Environment Full sun to partial or considerable shade.
Usually best in some shade. Tolerant to heat, salt spray
and to 15 or 20 degrees.

Pests Soil Mealybug. Slugs. Snails.

Propagation Division

Rate of Growth Slow to moderate

Pruning Cut to the ground in the spring, every few years.
Recovers slowly. Spreads by stolons, and by rhizomes
which are almost tuberous.

Seasonal Value Foliage mostly, but the flowers are
attractive.

Shape Mounding, arching.

Spread Wide

Height 6 to 12 inches

Soil Best if fertile, with sufficient organic matter and
moisture.

Use Ground cover. Erosion control. Indoors. Planters.

Origin Japan. Korea.

Comments Former names include *Mondo japonicum.*
Convallaria japonica and *Liriope japonica. Ophiopogon*
means Snakes Beard, probably referring to the
inflorescence. There is a cultivar with foliage that is
variegated.

Osteospermum fruticosum

Family Compositae

Leaves Evergreen. An herbaceous perennial or somewhat woody. Alternate. Sparsely toothed. Shape varying from elliptic to obovate or oblanceolate or spatulate. Nearly glabrous or sparsely-hairy and also glandular-dotted both sides. Ciliate. Medium green. Coriaceous. 2 to 4 inches long. 1/2 to one inch wide. Stems glabrous to hairy. Glandular-dotted and somewhat reddish.

Flowers White, or other colors with the different cultivars. Disc flowers purplish. Ray flowers white above, purplish below, or varying from this. In heads. To 2 inches across. Profuse. Regular. Corolla 5-lobed. Stamens 5. Most of year, especially winter through spring. Solitary or in loose panicles.

Fruit A glabrous, obovoid, 3-angled achene. With no pappus. 1/4 inch long.

Environment Full sun. Tolerant to seacoast conditions. To 20 or 30 degrees.

Pests Aphids

Propagation Seed. Cuttings. Self-layering.

Rate of Growth Rapid

Pruning Keep under control. Removing dead flowers encourages more bloom. Invasisve.

Seasonal Value Foliage. Flowers.

Shape Trailing, sprawling.

Spread Wide

Height 10 to 12 inches

Soil Tolerant to soils and to drought, but best with some water.

Use Ground cover. Containers. Erosion control. Hanging baskets. Slopes. Over walls.

Origin South Africa

Comments Once was *Dimorphotheca fruticosa*. *Osteospermum* means bone and seed, referring to the hard achene. Said to be fire-resistant.

207

Pachysandra terminalis

JAPANESE SPURGE
JAPANESE PACHYSANDRA

Family Buxaceae

Leaves Evergreen. An herbaceous perennial. Alternate or whorled. Dentate, especially towards the apex. Obovate. Conspicuously veined. Glandular-dotted both sides and either glabrous both sides or finely pubescent below. Dark green. Cuneate. Revolute. 2 to 4 inches long. To one inch or more wide. Stems finely hairy, with reddish striations.

Flowers White. To 1/2 inch long. In erect, terminal spikes which are 3 to 4 inches long and to one inch across. Regular. Petals none. Stamens 4. The staminate flowers are above and the pistillate are below. May.

Fruit A white, translucent, 3-pointed capsule, or sometimes drupaceous. 1/4 inch across. In the fall.

Environment Best in the shade. Tolerant to considerable shade. Not for hot, dry areas. To below zero.

Pests Greedy and Ivy Scale. Mites. Nematodes. Fungus Leaf Spot.

Propagation Cuttings. Division.

Rate of Growth Slow to moderate.

Pruning Cut back lightly in the spring before new growth starts. Not tolerant to severe pruning. Spreads by rhizomes, but not too aggressive.

Seasonal Value Foliage. Flowers.

Shape Compact. Erect.

Spread Wide

Height 8 to 10 inches

Soil Best if fertile and on the moist side. Acid.

Use Ground cover. Containers. Slopes.

Origin Japan

Comments *Pachysandra* means thick stamens. The flowers of this plant attract bees. Introduced about 1882. Much used in some areas where it probably grows faster than in the western region. There is a variegated form.

Pelargonium peltatum

Family Geraniaceae

Leaves Evergreen. Alternate. Shallowly 5-lobed. Lobes pointed. Entire. Broadly ovate or orbicular. Veining conspicuous. Glabrous and glandular-dotted both sides. Ciliate. Light to medium green. Coriaceous. 2 to 3 inches across and as long. Stems squarish, glandular-dotted and rough. Also sparsely hairy.

Flowers Variously-colored. In axillary umbels. 5 to 7-flowered. Each inflorescence about 2 to 3 inches across. On long stems. Regular. Petals 5. Stamens 10. Most of the year in coastal areas.

Fruit 5-valved and shaped as a stork's bill.

Environment Full sun or partial shade. Tolerant to wind and to seaside conditions.

Pests Aphids. Caterpillars. Crown Rot. Mosaic. Slugs. Snails.

Propagation Cuttings

Rate of Growth Rapid

Pruning Keep under control. Cut back as needed, but not until after frost danger.

Seasonal Value Foliage. Flowers.

Shape Sprawling

Spread 2 to 3 feet or more.

Height To 2 feet

Soil Fertile, moist soil is best, but tolerant to soils and to drought.

Use Ground cover. Containers. Hanging baskets. Slopes.

Origin South Africa

Comments Was once *Geranium peltatum*. *Pelargonium* means stork's bill, from the shape of the fruit. *peltatum* means shield-shaped, referring to the shape of the leaf. There are many cultivars.

211

Pennisetum setaceum

FOUNTAIN GRASS

Family Gramineae

Leaves Evergreen. An herbaceous perennial. Basal. Margins sharply serrate. Narrowly linear. Striated and glandular-dotted. Apparently glabrous. Medium green. To over 3 feet long.

Flowers Somewhat fuzzy spikes of rose-purple or copper-colored inflorescence. Somewhat nodding. To 14 inches long. Summer.

Fruit A grain

Environment Full sun or partial shade. Tolerant to hot, windy areas. To below zero.

Pests Soil Mealybug

Propagation Seed. Division. Cuttings. Self-sows.

Rate of Growth Rapid

Pruning Keep under control. Invasive. Remove dead inflorescence.

Seasonal Value Foliage. Inflorescence.

Shape Erect, with a nodding inflorescence.

Spread Wide

Height To 3 1/2 or 4 feet

Soil Tolerant to soils and to drought.

Use Ground cover. Containers. Group plantings. For dry arrangements.

Origin Africa

Comments Formerly *P. ruppelii* or *P. ruppelianum*. *setaceum* means bristlelike. Cultivars include 'Atrosanguineum', 'Cupreum' and 'Rubrum'.

Pernettya mucronata

Family   Ericaceae

Leaves   Evergreen. Alternate. Serrate. Cuspidate. Ovate. Somewhat revolute. Dark glossy green. Glabrous and glandular-dotted both sides. Midrib conspicuous. Some leaves turn bronzy in cool weather. About 1/2 inch long. To 1/4 inch wide. Stems finely hairy. Reddish on upper side. About 1/8 inch wide.

Flowers   White to pink. Urceolate. 1/4 inch long. Corolla gamopetalous and 5-lobed. Stamens 10. Regular. Spring-summer.

Fruit   A metallic appearing berry. 5-valved. Purple, white, red, rose-pink or nearly black. Persisting from fall until spring.

Environment   Full sun. Partial shade where warm. To zero degrees.

Pests   Aphids. Mites.

Propagation   Seed. Cuttings. Layering.

Rate of Growth   Rapid

Pruning   Keep under control. Invasive. Prune back as needed for best appearance. Spreads by rhizomes.

Seasonal Value   Foliage. Flowers. Winter color (Fruit).

Shape   Clumping

Spread   Wide

Height   2 to 3 feet

Soil   Acid. Fertile. Moist.

Use   Ground cover. Borders. Containers. Low hedge.

Origin   Straits of Magellan to Chile.

Comments   Formerly *P. rupicola* and *Arbutus mucronata*. *mucronata* refers to the word mucro, a spiny tip. Cultivars include 'Alba', 'Coccinea', 'Rosea' and 'Rubra'.

Phlox subulata

Family Polemoniaceae

Leaves Evergreen. An herbaceous perennial. Mostly opposite, while the upper ones may be alternate. Entire. Linear to subulate. Crowded. Glabrous and glandular-dotted both sides. Ciliate. Medium green. To one inch long. About 1/8 inch wide. Stems reddish or brownish, squarish and hairy.

Flowers Various shades of pink, red and purplish. To 3/4 inch across. Salverform. In terminal panicles. Profuse. Regular. Petals 5. Stamens 5. Spring-summer.

Fruit A small capsule.

Environment Full sun. To below zero.

Pests Aphids. Mites. Crown Rot. Fungus Leaf Spot. Aster Yellows. Mildew. Rust. Verticillium Wilt.

Propagation Best from division. Variation from seed.

Rate of Growth Rapid

Pruning Cut back after flowering. Keep under control.

Seasonal Value Foliage. Flowers.

Shape Mat-forming

Spread Wide

Height To 6 inches

Soil Tolerant to soils and somewhat to drought, but best with some water. Provide good drainage.

Use Ground cover. Borders. Rock gardens. Over walls.

Origin New York to Maryland, west to Michigan.

Comments Was formerly *P. setacea*. *Phlox* means flame. *subulata* means awl-shaped. There are numerous cultivars.

217

Phyla nodiflora

GARDEN LIPPIA

Family Verbenaceae

Leaves Evergreen. An herbaceous perennial. Opposite. Toothed, especially toward the apex. Spatulate, cuneate or obovate. Coarsely hairy and glandular-dotted both sides. Grayish-green to green. To 1 3/4 inches long. To 1/4 inch wide. Stems hairy.

Flowers Lilac to rose-colored. In dense heads which are to 1/2 inch across. Axillary. Irregular. Corolla with 2 unequal lips. Stamens 4. Spring-fall.

Fruit Dry. Consisting of 2 nutlets.

Environment Full sun. Tolerant to heat and to salt spray and to desert conditions. From 20 to 30 degrees.

Pests Mites. Root Knot Nematode

Propagation Seed. Cuttings. Division. Self-sows.

Rate of Growth Moderate to rapid

Pruning Keep under control. Can be mowed. Remove flowers to discourage bees. Spreads by stolons and by rhizomes.

Seasonal Value Foliage. Flowers.

Shape Mat-forming

Spread Wide

Height One to 3 inches

Soil Tolerant to soils and to drought, but best with some water.

Use Ground cover. Planting strips. Slopes.

Origin From many tropical and subtropical regions.

Comments Was once named *Lippia nodiflora*. *Phyla* refers to the dense flower heads. *nodiflora* means with flowers at the nodes. This plant is a very variable species.

218

Polygonum capitatum

ROSE CARPET KNOTWEED

Family Polygonaceae

Leaves Evergreen. An herbaceous perennial. Alternate. Entire. Elliptic. With reddish-brown markings. Glandular-dotted and pubescent both sides. Ciliate. Mature leaves a dark green. To 1 1/2 inches long. One inch wide. Stems reddish and hairy, jointed. To about 12 inches long.

Flowers Pink. In dense heads, forming racemes. Heads to 1/2 inch or more across. Regular. Petals none.   ns Stamens 8. Most of the year.

Fruit A lenticular or 3-angled achene.

Environment Full sun or partial shade. Usually best in the sun. To about 30 degrees.

Pests Aphids. Slugs. Snails.

Propagation Seed. Division. Self-sows.

Rate of Growth Rapid

Pruning Keep under control. Spreads by seed and by stolons. Very invasive. Cut back periodically.

Seasonal Value Foliage. Flowers.

Shape Mat-forming

Spread Wide

Height 2 to 6 inches

Soil Best when acid, moist and well-drained. Tolerant to drought, but best with some water.

Use Ground cover. Containers. Hanging baskets. Rock gardens. Over walls.

Origin The Himalayas

Comments *Polygonum* means many-kneed, referring to the jointed stems. *capitatum* means with heads, in reference to the flowers.

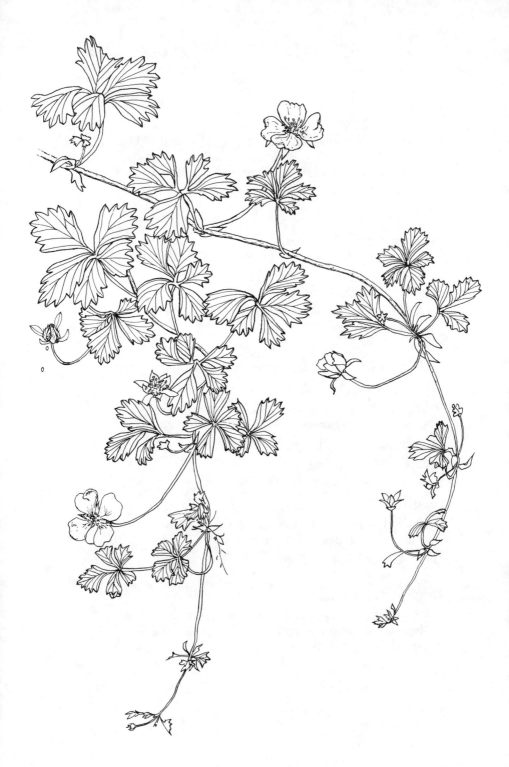

221

Potentilla tabernaemontanii

Family Rosaceae

Leaves Evergreen. An herbaceous perennial. Alternate or basal. Palmately compound, with 5 leaflets. Each leaflet dentate or nearly lobed. Obovate to cuneate. Alternate or basal. Glandular-dotted both sides. Glabrous above, sparsely hairy below. Ciliate. Medium green. To 3/4 inch long and about 1/2 inch wide. Stems weak, hairy.

Flowers Yellow. about one inch across. In loose cymes, with 3 to 5 flowers in each cluster. Regular. Petals 5. Stamens numerous. Spring and summer.

Fruit A dry achene.

Environment Full sun or partial shade. Shade where warm. To below zero.

Pests Aphids. Mites. Rust.

Propagation Seed. Division. Self-layering.

Rate of Growth Rapid

Pruning Keep under control. Spreads by stolons.

Seasonal Value Foliage. Flowers.

Shape Mat-forming. Trailing.

Spread Wide

Height 3 to 6 inches

Soil Tolerant to soils and to drought, but best with some water and with good drainage.

Use Ground cover. Between stepping stones.

Origin Europe

Comments *Potentilla* means powerful, referring to the medicinal properties of this plant. Has been named *P. verna* and *P. verna 'Nana'*.

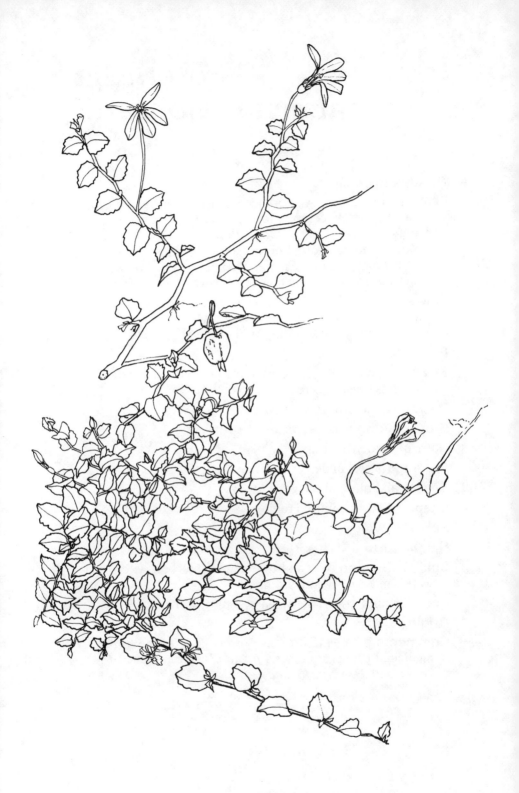

Pratia angulata

Family Lobeliaceae

Leaves Evergreen. An herbaceous perennial. Alternate. Dentate. Nearly orbicular. Glabrous and glandular-dotted both sides. 1/2 inch long and about as wide. Medium, dull green. Stems somewhat reddish, glandular-dotted and with a longitudinal groove.

Flowers White, with purple veins, or bluish-white. 3/4 inch across. On stems 2 inches long. Solitary and axillary. Irregular, with 2 petals being shorter than the other 3. Corolla 5-lobed. Stamens 5. Spring-summer.

Fruit A reddish-purple berry. 1/4 inch across. Winter.

Environment Full sun. Partial shade where warm. Usually best in some shade. 30 to 40 degrees.

Pests Aphids. Mites.

Propagation. Seed. Division.

Rate of Growth Rapid

Pruning Keep under control. Cut back in the fall or in the spring. Spreads by stolons.

Seasonal Value Foliage. Flowers. Fruit (winter).

Shape Mat-forming. Trailing.

Spread Wide

Height 2 to 6 inches

Soil Fertile, with sufficient water.

Use Ground cover. Between stones. Rock gardens.

Origin New Zealand

Comments Somewhat similar to *Laurentia fluviatilis;* however, the latter has flowers which are nearly regular, the leaves are pubescent, at least when young. Also, the stems are hairy.

Prunus laurocerasus 'Zabeliana'

ZABEL LAUREL
ZABEL CHERRY LAUREL

Family Rosaceae

Leaves Evergreen. Alternate. Entire. Mostly lanceolate. Revolute. Prominent midrib. Glabrous and glandular-dotted both sides. Dark glossy green. 4 to 5 inches long. To one inch in width. Somewhat cuspidate. Stems glabrous and glandular-dotted.

Flowers White. Each about 3/8 inch across. In erect racemes which are to 1 1/4 inches or more in length. Regular. Petals 5. Stamens numerous. Late spring and summer.

Fruit A dark purple drupe.

Environment Tolerant to more sun than the parent plant, but doing best in some shade. From zero to 10 degrees.

Pests Mites. Thrips.

Propagation Cuttings

Rate of Growth Moderate

Pruning Only as needed to keep a desired shape.

Seasonal Value Foliage. Flowers.

Shape Low. Compact. Branches arching.

Spread To 4 feet

Height 3 to 6 feet

Soil Tolerant, but best with some moisture and with good drainage.

Use Ground cover. Espalier. Foundation.

Origin Parent plant is from Asia and Europe.

Comments A clean-appearing plant in the landscape if the pests are kept under control. These may be more injurious when the plant is under stress from lack of moisture.

Pyracantha koidzumi
'Santa Cruz'

SANTA CRUZ PYRACANTHA

Family Rosaceae

Leaves Evergreen. Alternate. Serrate toward the apex. Oblanceolate and obtuse. Revolute. Glandular-dotted and either glabrous or sparsely pubescent both sides. Medium green. Emarginate to cuspidate. 1 1/2 to 2 1/2 inches long. To 3/4 inch wide. Stems reddish and pubescent. Spines to 1/2 inch or more in length.

Flowers White. Fragrant. Each to 1/4 inch across. In corymbs. Regular. Petals 4 to 5. Stamens numerous. Spring.

Fruit A red pome (berry). To 1/4 inch across. Edible, but not especially tasty. Winter period.

Environment Full sun. To 10 degrees.

Pests Aphids. Kuno Scale. Fire Blight. Mites. Woolly Apple Aphid.

Propagation Cuttings. Layering.

Rate of Growth Rapid

Pruning As needed to keep desired shape.

Seasonal Value Foliage. Flowers. Fragrance (Flowers). Winter color (Fruit).

Shape Low. Stiff. Branching.

Spread 4 to 6 feet

Height To 3 feet or more

Soil Tolerant to soils and to drought, but best with some water.

Use Ground cover. Barrier plant. Informal hedge. Slopes.

Origin Formosa

Comments The parent plant was once *P. formosana*. *Pyracantha* means fire and thorn. Often used as the common name for *Pyracantha spp* is the name Firethorn.

228

Rosmarinus officinalis '*Prostratus*'

DWARF ROSEMARY

Family Labiatae

Leaves Evergreen. Opposite. Entire. Linear. Obtuse. Revolute. Veining conspicuous above. Dark, glossy green above. White tomentose below. Presenting a grayish appearance. Aromatic. 1/2 to over one inch long. To 1/8 inch wide. Stems squarish and white hairy.

Flowers Pale lavender blue. 1/2 inch across. In few-flowered verticillasters. Arranged in short, axillary racemes. Fragrant. Irregular. Corolla 5-lobed. Stamens 2. February to May and most of the year.

Fruit Consisting of 4 glabrous nutlets.

Environment Full sun. Tolerant to heat and to desert conditions. To 10 degrees or lower.

Pests Aphids

Propagation Cuttings

Rate of Growth Slow to moderate

Pruning Keep under control. Cut to laterals.

Seasonal Value Foliage. Flowers. Fragrance (Foliage, Flowers).

Shape Sprawling. Compact.

Spread 4 to 5 feet or more.

Height To 2 feet

Soil Tolerant to soils and to drought, but best with some water. Needs good drainage.

Use Ground cover. Containers. Erosion control. Slopes. Over walls.

Origin The Mediterranean region

Comments *Rosmarinus* means Sea-Dew, referring to the fact that the parent plant was common along the coast of southern France. Said to be fire-resistant if irrigated periodically. Much used in cooking, for medicinal purposes and for perfumery. Used for tea and for wine. Rosemary was thought to bring good fortune and to restore one's memory. Other cultivars include 'Albus', 'Collingwood Ingram', 'Lockwood de Forest', 'Tuscan Blue'.

Sagina subulata 'Aurea'

Family   Caryophyllaceae

Leaves   Evergreen. An herbaceous perennial. Opposite. Entire. Subulate to linear. Aristate. Glabrous and glandular-dotted both sides. Yellowish to yellow-green. To 1/4 inch long.

Flowers   White. 3/16 inch or more across. Mostly solitary and terminal. Petals 5. Stamens 10. Regular. Summer.

Fruit   A 4 to 5-valved capsule. 1/8 inch long.

Environment   Full sun or partial shade. Shade where warm. To below zero.

Pests   Crown Rot. Slugs. Snails.

Propagation   Seed. Division.

Rate of Growth   Rapid

Pruning   Keep under control. Somewhat invasive. Spreading by stolons.

Seasonal Value   Foliage

Shape   Mat-forming

Spread   Wide

Height   3 to 4 inches

Soil   Fertile, with sufficient moisture.

Use   Ground cover. Between stones. For small areas.

Origin   Europe

Comments   Formerly *Spergula pilifera*. Sometimes named *Arenaria verna*. Irish Moss and *Arenaria verna 'Aurea'*. Scotch Moss. Where the flowers are mostly solitary with *Sagina,* they are in clusters with *Arenaria*. The word *subulata* means awl-shaped, referring to the leaf shape.

233

Santolina chamaecyparissus

Family Compositae

Leaves Evergreen. Alternate. Entire. Pinnately divided into narrow segments. Each segment about 1/8 inch long. Cylindrical. White tomentose all over. White. Aromatic. To 1 1/2 inches long. Stems with stiff, white hairs.

Flowers Yellow. In globular heads. Each to 3/4 inch across. Solitary. Profuse. On long peduncles. Regular. Corolla 4 to 5-lobed. Stamens 4 or 5. Summer.

Fruit A 3-angled, glabrous achene. No pappus.

Environment Full sun. 10 to 20 degrees or lower.

Pests Aphids. Black Scale.

Propagation Seed. Cuttings.

Rate of Growth Rapid

Pruning Head back after flowering. Makes for a neater-looking plant and also helps to control the woodiness.

Seasonal Value Foliage. Flowers. Fragrance (Foliage).

Shape Round and compact. Stiff.

Spread One to 2 feet

Height To 2 feet

Soil Tolerant to soils and to drought.

Use Ground cover. Dry arrangements. Low hedge. Herb gardens. Slopes. Over walls.

Origin Mediterranean

Comments Formerly *S. incana* and *S. tomentosa*. The word *chamaecyparissus* means dwarf Cypress, since the leaves somewhat resemble those of Cypress. Has been used as an herb, for moth-proofing and in Potpourri. Said to be fire-resistant. *Santolina virens* is a dark green color. Cultivars include 'Nana' and 'Plumosus'.

Sarcococca hookerana var. humilis

SMALL HIMALAYAN SARCOCOCCA

Family Buxaceae

Leaves Evergreen. Alternate. Entire. Elliptic to lanceolate. Coriaceous. Glabrous both sides. Dark, glossy green. One to 3 inches long. 1/2 to 3/4 inch in width.

Flowers White. In short, 4-flowered racemes. Axillary. Hidden in the foliage. Fragrant. Male flowers borne above the female. Regular. Petals none. Stamens usually 4. Fall and winter.

Fruit Bluish-black. Glossy. Drupelike. 1/2 inch across. Fall and winter.

Environment Partial shade best. Tolerant to considerable shade. To below zero.

Pests Black, Greedy and Hemispherical Scales.

Propagation Seed. Cuttings. Division.

Rate of Growth Slow

Pruning Keep under control. Spreads by rhizomes.

Seasonal Value Foliage. Flowers. Fragrance (Flowers). Fall color (Flowers and fruit).

Shape Compact. Erect. Stiff.

Spread 8 feet or more

Height To 1 1/2 feet

Soil Best when acid, organic and moist. Keep moist at least until established.

Use Ground cover. Containers. Entryways. For shaded areas.

Origin China

Comments Sometimes spelled *hookeriana* in the past. Also named *S. humilis* previously. *Sarcococca* means fleshy and berry, referring to the fruit.

237

Saxifraga stolonifera

Family Saxifragaceae

Leaves Evergreen. An herbaceous perennial. Basal. Stem leaves alternate. Crenate to dentate. Orbicular or cordate. Veins on upper side conspicuous because of grayish coloring. Sparsely hairy upper side, glabrous below. Glandular-dotted both sides. Warty and reddish below. Ciliate, with pink hairs. Grayish to green above. 2 to 4 inches across and as long. Petioles long, pink hairy.

Flowers White. To one inch across. In panicles. Irregular, with 2 petals much longer than the other 3. Stamens 10. spring and summer.

Fruit A 2-beaked capsule.

Environment Best in partial shade. 20 to 30 degrees.

Pests Aphids. Soil Mealybugs. Slugs. Snails. White Fly.

Propagation Division

Rate of Growth Rapid

Pruning Keep under control. Aggressive. Spreading by long, thin stolons, at the ends of which new plants form.

Seasonal Value Foliage. Flowers.

Shape Tufted. Trailing.

Spread Wide

Height 6 to 8 inches or more

Soil Fertile soil best, with sufficient moisture and good drainage.

Use Ground cover. Containers. Hanging baskets. Indoors. Rock gardens.

Origin Asia

Comments Formerly named *S. sarmentosa* and before that *Sekika sarmentosa*. *Saxifraga* means rock-breaking. *stolonifera* means with stolons. 'Tricolor' is a cultivar.

Sedum acre

GOLDMOSS SEDUM

Family Crassulaceae

Leaves Evergreen. An herbaceous perennial. Succulent. Alternate. Entire. Ovoid and terete. Imbricated. Glandular-dotted and glabrous all around, but not papillose. Light to yellowish-green. 3/16 inch or less in length. About 1/16 inch wide. Stems glabrous and glandular-dotted.

Flowers Bright yellow. Each to 1/2 inch across. In terminal cymes. Regular. Petals 5. Stamens 10. Spring-summer.

Fruit Wide-spreading follicles.

Environment Full sun or partial shade. Tolerant to considerable shade. To below zero.

Pests Aphids. Mealybug.

Propagation Cuttings. Division.

Rate of Growth Rapid

Pruning Keep under control. Invasive.

Seasonal Value Foliage. Flowers.

Shape Procumbent. Mat-forming.

Spread Wide

Height 2 to 5 inches

Soil Tolerant to soils and to drought, but best with some water.

Use Ground cover. Borders. Between stepping stones. Indoors. Over walls.

Origin Europe. North Africa. West Asia.

Comments *Sedum* is from a word meaning to sit, because of the way in which some species grow upon rocks. Also the word means to assuage, from the healing properties of some species. The leaves have a peppery taste. This plant has naturalized in the north. Cultivars include ''Majus' and 'Minus'.

Sedum brevifolium

GREEN STONECROP

Family   Crassulaceae

Leaves   Evergreen. An herbaceous perennial. Succulent. Alternate or opposite. 4 or 5-ranked. Nearly globular or ovoid. Entire. Glabrous and glandular-dotted all around. A chalky gray or green color. Often suffused with red. 1/8 to 1/2 inch long. About 1/8 inch wide. Stems glabrous and glandular-dotted. Somewhat striated.

Flowers   White to pinkish, but mostly white. Each to 1/4 inch or more across. Profuse. In terminal, few-flowered cymes. Regular. Petals 5. Stamens 10. Attractive to bees. Spring and summer.

Fruit   A follicle

Environment   Full sun or partial shade. Tolerant to considerable shade. To below zero.

Pests   Aphids. Mealybug.

Propagation   Seed. Cuttings.

Rate of Growth   Rapid

Pruning   Keep under control. Very aggressive. Each part can root (this is true of most succulents).

Seasonal Value   Foliage. Flowers.

Shape   Dense. Low. Mat-forming.

Spread   Wide

Height   3 to 4 inches

Soil   Tolerant to soils and to drought, but best with some water.

Use   Ground cover. Border. Indoors. Between stepping stones. Rock gardens.

Origin   Northwest Africa. Europe.

Comemnts   Sometimes grown as *S. pittonei 'Album'*, which is not correct. *brevifolium* refers to the short leaves.

Sedum confusum

MEXICAN SEDUM

Family Crassulaceae

Leaves Evergreen. An herbaceous perennial. Succulent. Entire. Alternate to whorled. Obovate to lanceolate. Not terete. Glandular-dotted and glabrous both sides. Light, yellowish-green. Tinged with red. To 3/4 inch long. To 1/2 inch wide. Nearly emarginate. Stems glabrous.

Flowers Yellow. Stellate. Each to 3/4 inch across. In terminal cymes. Regular. Petals 5. Stamens 10. Spring-summer.

Fruit A follicle

Environment Full sun or partial shade. Tolerant to considerable shade. To 25 degrees.

Pests Aphids. Mealybug.

Propagation Seed. Cuttings.

Rate of Growth Moderate to rapid

Pruning Remove dead flowers. Thin periodically. Keep under control.

Seasonal Value Foliage. Flowers.

Shape Low. Decumbent.

Spread Wide

Height 8 to 12 inches

Soil Tolerant to soils and to drought, but best with some water.

Use Ground cover. Containers. Indoors. Rock gardens. Slopes.

Origin Mexico

Comments Formerly named *Sedum amecamecanum*. Often used to cover fairly large areas very effectively.

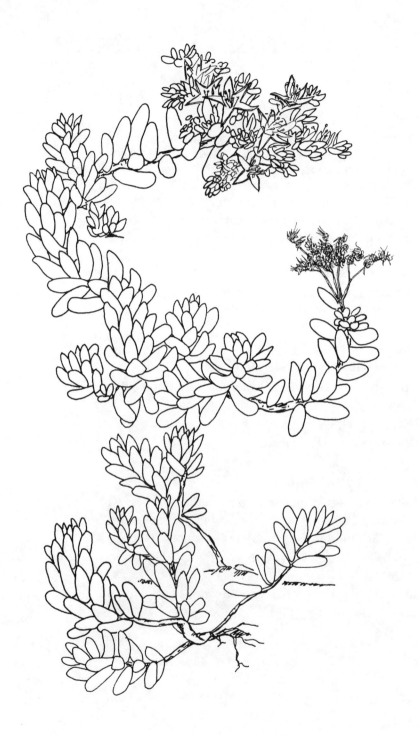

Sedum rubrotinctum

Family Crassulaceae

Leaves Evergreen. An herbaceous perennial. Succulent. Alternate. Entire. Oblong. Terete. Glabrous and glandular-dotted all around. Green, with reddish-brown tips. Often bronzy-red in the sun. 3/4 inch long. About 1/4 inch wide.

Flowers Reddish-yellow. Each to 1/2 inch across. In terminal cymes. Regular. Petals 5. Stamens 10. Spring and summer.

Fruit Follicles

Environment Full sun or partial shade. Tolerant to considerable shade. To 25 degrees.

Pests Aphids. Mealybug.

Propagation Seed. Cuttings.

Rate of Growth Rapid

Pruning Thin as needed. Keep under control. Invasive.

Seasonal Value Foliage. Flowers.

Shape Decumbent. Sprawling.

Spread 12 inches or more

Height 6 to 8 inches or more

Soil Tolerant to soils and to drought, but best with come water.

Use Ground cover. Containers. Rock gardens. Hanging basekts. Indoors.

Origin Said to be a garden hybrid. Parentage unknown.

Comments Has been mis-named *S. guatemalense*.

Senecio cineraria

Family Compositae

Leaves Evergreen. Alternate and basal. Pinnately-lobed. With oblong and obtuse segments. Revolute. Gray to whitish-tomentose both sides. Becoming greenish above. 6 to 8 inches long. 2 to 4 inches wide. Stems white-tomentose.

Flowers Yellow. Heads 1 1/2 inches across. In compound, terminal corymbs which are 2 to 3 inches or more across. Regular. Corolla 4 to 5-lobed. Stamens 4 or 5. Summer.

Fruit An achene, with soft white pappus.

Environment Full sun. To below zero.

Pests Aphids

Propagation Seed. Cuttings.

Rate of Growth Rapid

Pruning Head back periodically to control. A vigorous grower.

Seasonal Value Foliage. Flowers.

Shape Sprawling. Compact. Upright.

Spread 2 to 4 feet

Height 2 to 2½ feet

Soil Tolerant to soils and to drought. Best with occasional watering.

Use Ground cover. Rock gardens.

Origin Mediterranean area

Comments Formerly *Cineraria maritima* and *S. acantifolius. Senecio* means old man, referring to the hoary pappus. *cineraria* means ash, referring to the color of the foliage. This is said to be a fire-resistant plant, if watered periodically.

Soleirolia soleirolii

BABY'S TEARS

Family Urticaceae

Leaves Evergreen. An herbaceous perennial. Alternate. Entire. Nearly orbicular. Sparsely hairy both sides. Glandular-dotted both sides. Light green. Glossy above. Almost 1/4 inch long and nearly as wide. Stems delicate, hairy, pinkish.

Flowers White to greenish. Very small and not readily visible. Solitary and axillary. Regular. Petals zero. Stamens 4.

Fruit An ovoid achene.

Environment Partial, to considerable shade. To about 25 degrees.

Pests Slugs. Snails.

Propagation Division. Self-layers.

Rate of Growth Rapid

Pruning Keep under control. Aggressive. Spreads by stolons.

Seasonal Value Foliage

Shape Mat-forming

Spread Wide

Height 2 to 3 inches

Soil Fertile, moist and well-drained.

Use Ground cover. Between stepping stones. For shaded areas.

Origin The Mediterranean area

Comments Was once *Helxine soleirolii*. Sometimes considered to be a weed.

Sollya heterophylla

Family   Pittosporaceae

Leaves   Evergreen. Alternate. Entire. Lanceolate to oblong to ovate. Acute. Glabrous and glandular-dotted both sides. Midrib conspicuous. Dark, glossy green above. From one to 2 inches long. 1/2 to 3/4 inch in width. Stems glabrous and reddish.

Flowers   Brilliant blue. Campanulate. Pendulous. In terminal or axillary cymes. Profuse. Each flower 1/3 to 1/2 inch long. Most of the summer.

Fruit   Blue. 1/3 to 1/2 inch long.

Environment   Full sun to partial shade. Some shade usually best. Tolerant to heat and to some wind, but not tolerant to severe cold or heat. 20 to 30 degrees.

Pests   Aphids. Scale.

Propagation   Seed. Cuttings.

Rate of Growth   Moderate

Pruning   Can be thinned annually.

Seasonal Value   Foliage. Flowers.

Shape   Trailing, twining. Mat-forming.

Spread   5 to 6 feet

Height   5 to 6 feet

Soil   Best in a fertile soil. Drought-tolerant once established, but best with some water.

Use   Ground cover. Border. Hanging baskets. Slopes. Semi-vine.

Origin   Australia

Comemnts   Was once *Sollya fusiformis*. Was also *Billardiera fusiformis. heterophylla* means with different kinds of leaves, meaning the latter are variable on this plant.

253

Stachys byzantina

WOOLLY LAMB'S EARS
LAMB'S EARS

Family Labiatae

Leaves Evergreen. An herbaceous perennial. Opposite. Crenate to dentate. White tomentose both sides and on stems. Silky-white. 4 to 6 inches long. About one inch wide. Oblong to spatulate. Stems squarish.

Flowers Purple. Each about one inch long. In many-flowered verticillasters. Each of these is up to one foot in length. Irregular. Corolla 5-lobed. Stamens 4. June and July.

Fruit Consisting of 4 ovoid nutlets.

Environment Full sun best. While tolerant to zero degrees, it will appear quite ragged. Recovers with warmer weather.

Pests Aphids. Soil Mealybug.

Propagation Seed. Division.

Rate of Growth Moderate to rapid

Pruning Remove dead and discolored parts after the frost period. Keep under control.

Seasonal Value Foliage. Flowers.

Shape Decumbent. Mat-forming.

Spread To 3 feet or more

Height One to 1 1/2 feet

Soil Tolerant to soils and to some drought, but best with some water. Provide good drainage.

Use Ground cover. Borders. Rock gardens.

Origin Asia. Turkey.

Comments Was once named *S. lanata* and *S. olympica*. *byzantina* means from the byzantine or Turkish region.

Thymus praecox arcticus

Family Labiatae

Leaves Evergreen. An herbaceous perennial. Opposite. Entire. Obovate. Mostly glabrous, with the petioles and the stems being pubescent. Glandular-dotted both sides. Dark green. Aromatic. To 1/4 inch long. Nearly as wide.

Flowers Purplish-white. About 1/2 inch across. In verticillasters. Axillary. Irregular. Corolla 5-lobed. Stamens 4. Attractive to bees. June-September.

Fruit Consisting of 4 glabrous nutlets.

Environment Full sun. Tolerant to partial shade. To below zero.

Pests Aphids. Soil Mealybug. Slugs. Snails.

Propagation Seed. Cuttings. Division.

Rate of Growth Rapid

Pruning Keep under control. Spreads by stolons.

Seasonal Value Foliage. Flowers. Fragrance (Leaves).

Shape Mat-forming

Spread Wide

Height 2 to 6 inches

Soil Tolerant to soils and to drought. Should have good drainage.

Use Ground cover. Between stepping stones.

Origin Europe

Comments Formerly *T. serpyllum* or at least has been so named. *T. serpyllum* may not be in cultivation. The leaves of Thyme are used in Potpourri and for seasoning in cooking.

Thymus pseudolanuginosus

WOOLLY THYME

Family Labiatae

Leaves Evergreen. An herbaceous perennial. Opposite. Entire. Elliptic. White pubescent and glandular-dotted both sides. Grayish. Aromatic. 3/16 inch long and about 1/8 inch in width. The stems are hairy.

Flowers Pale pink. About 3/16 inch across. In verticillasters. Axillary. Irregular. Corolla 5-lobed. Stamens 4. Spring.

Fruit Consisting of 4 glabrous nutlets.

Environment Full sun. Tolerant to partial shade and to neglect. To below zero.

Pests Aphids. Soil Mealybug. Bees attracted to flowers.

Propagation Seed. Cuttings. Division.

Rate of Growth Rapid

Pruning Keep under control. Spreads by stolons.

Seasonal Value Foliage. Flowers. Fragrance (Leaves).

Shape Mat-forming

Spread Wide

Height 2 to 3 inches

Soil Tolerant, but best when dry and well-drained.

Use Ground cover. Containers. Between stepping stones. Over and in cracks in walls.

Origin Not known.

Comments Has been known as *T. lanuginosus*. The nomenclature of the Thymus species is somewhat confusing. Thyme is used in cooking.

Trachelospermum jasminoides

STAR JASMINE
CONFEDERATE JASMINE

Family Apocynaceae

Leaves Evergreen. Opposite. Entire. Elliptic to oblong or oblanceolate. Glabrous both sides. Dark green. Exuding a milky substance when any part is injured. To 3 inches long. About 3/4 to one inch in width.

Flowers White. Petals arranged as in a pinwheel. About 3/4 to one inch across. In axillary cymes. Very fragrant, especially at night. Regular. Corolla 5-lobed. Stamens 5. Summer.

Fruit A pair of slender, cylindrical follicles which are each 4 to 6 inches in length. Seeds have a tuft of white hairs at one end. The fruit is not commonly seen.

Environment Full sun to partial shade. More flowers in sun, but foliage is more yellow. Better color to foliage in shade, but fewer flowers. Tolerant to wind. 10 to 20 degrees.

Pests Black Scale. Mealybug. Mites. Oak Root Fungus.

Propagation Cuttings

Rate of Growth Moderate

Pruning Only to keep to desired shape.

Seasonal Value Foliage. Flowers. Fragrance (Flowers).

Shape Low. Compact or a vine.

Spread 4 to 5 feet

Height 1 1/2 to 2 feet or to 20 feet as a vine.

Soil Best when fertile, moist, with good drainage. Fertilize periodically.

Use Ground cover. Containers Espalier. Over walls.

Origin China

Comments At one time was *Rhynchospermum jasminoides*. *Trachelospermum* means neck and seed, referring to the seeds. If grown as a vine, it climbs by means of twining stems. It also produces holdfasts, with which to cling. There are several cultivars.

261

Tradescantia albiflora

Family   Commelinaceae

Leaves   Evergreen in temperate areas. An herbaceous perennial. Alternate. Entire. Oblong to elliptic. Leaves and stems striated. Glabrous and glandular-dotted both sides. Medium to dark green. 2 to 3 inches long. About one inch wide.

Flowers   White. 1/2 inch across. In umbels. Regular. Petals 3. Stamens 6. Each flower lasts but one day. Summer-Fall.

Fruit   A 3-valved capsule.

Environment   Best in partial shade. Tolerant to considerable shade. 20 to 30 degrees.

Pests   Aphids. White Flies. Slugs. Snails. Leaf Spot.

Propagation   Cuttings. Layering.

Rate of Growth   Rapid

Pruning   Keep under control. Aggressive. Spreads by stolons.

Seasonal Value   Foliage. Flowers.

Shape   Decumbent to erect. Trailing.

Spread   Wide

Height   10 to 12 inches or more.

Soil   Best if fertile and with sufficient moisture.

Use   Ground cover. Containers. Hanging baskets. Indoors. For shaded areas.

Origin   South America

Comments   Has been confused with *T. fluminensis,* but the latter has leaves which are purplish below. *T. andersoniana* is Common Spiderwort. Cultivars of *T. albiflora* include: 'Albovittata', 'Aurea', 'Laekensis', 'Variegata'.

Verbena peruviana

Family Verbenaceae

Leaves Evergreen. An herbaceous perennial. Opposite. Serrate or dentate. Oblong to lanceolate or ovate. Pubescent both sides. Scabrous. Medium-green. One to 2 inches long. About 1/2 inch wide. Stems squarish and pubescent.

Flowers Bright red. Cultivar colors vary. About 1/2 inch across. In somewhat flat, capitate spikes which are solitary on the long peduncles. Irregular. Corolla 5-lobed. Stamens 4. All summer.

Fruit Comprised of 4 nutlets.

Environment Full sun. Tolerant to heat. To 27 degrees.

Pests Aphids. Soil Mealybug. White Flies. Nematodes. Botrytis.

Propagation Seed. Cuttings. Self-layering (Stolons).

Rate of Growth Rapid

Pruning Keep under control. Spreads by stolons. Vigorous.

Seasonal Value Foliage. Flowers.

Shape Erect. Sprawling. Trailing.

Spread 2 feet or more

Height 6 to 8 inches

Soil Tolerant to soils and to drought. Irrigate only infrequently. Provide good drainage. Fertilize periodically.

Use Ground cover. Borders. Group planting. Erosion control.

Origin Argentina to Brazil

Comments Former names include *Erinus peruviana, Glandularia peruviana, Verbena chamaedryfolia.* There are many cultivars. Has naturalized in some areas such as Florida. Several species have pinnatified leaves, including some cultivars.

Veronica repens

Family Scrophulariaceae

Leaves Evergreen. An herbaceous perennial. Opposite, or whorled. Dentate. Ovate. Pubescent both sides. Also glandular-dotted both sides. Ciliate. Medium green. 1/2 to one inch long. About 1/4 inch wide. With weak, pubescent stems.

Flowers Bluish, lavender or white. Solitary or in few-flowered, terminal racemes. Each flower about ¼ inch across. Irregular. Corolla 4 to 5-lobed. Stamens 2. February-March.

Fruit A flattened, notched, brownish capsule.

Environment Full sun or partial shade. To below zero.

Pests Mites. Soil Mealybug.

Propagation Seed. Division.

Rate of Growth Rapid

Pruning Keep under control. Aggressive. Spreading by stolons.

Seasonal Value Foliage. Flowers.

Shape Mat-forming

Spread Wide

Height 3/4 to 4 inches

Soil Best if fertile, moist, well-drained. Needs moisture during the summer.

Use Ground cover. Between stepping stones. Along sunny borders.

Origin Corsica. Spain.

Comments *Veronica* is from St. Veronica. This plant is not tolerant to traffic. It can be a weed in turf areas. Cultivars include 'Alba' and 'Rosea'.

267

Viburnum davidii

Family   Caprifoliaceae

Leaves   Evergreen. Opposite. Entire, or sometimes slightly toothed. Conspicuously net-veined and also conspicuously 3-veined from the base. Elliptic. Glabrous and glandular-dotted both sides. Revolute. Medium to dark green. To 6 inches long and 1 1/2 to 2 inches in width.

Flowers   White. Buds are pink. In dense, peduncled cymes which are to 3 inches across. Corolla rotate and 5-lobed. Stamens 5. Regular. Early summer.

Fruit   A metallic blue drupe. More fruit seen in group plantings.

Environment   Full sun in cooler areas. Best where cool. Does well in northern California. Best in some shade. To 10 degrees or lower.

Pests   Mites. Thrips. Leaf Spot. Mildew. Rust.

Propagation   Seed. Cuttings.

Rate of Growth   Moderate

Pruning   Only if needed.

Seasonal Value   Foliage. Flowers. Fruit.

Shape   Low. Compact.

Spread   3 to 4 feet

Height   To 3 feet

Soil   Best when fertile, acid, moist and well-drained.

Use   Ground cover. Planter boxes. Strips.

Origin   China

Comments   An effective ground cover in a favorable environment.

Vinca major

Family   Apocynaceae

Leaves   Evergreen. An herbaceous perennial. Opposite. Entire. Ovate. Glabrous and glandular-dotted both sides. Ciliate. Dark glossy green. Truncate to sub-cordate at base. 2 to 3 inches long and to one inch in width.

Flowers   Bright blue. One to 2 inches across. Solitary and axillary. Regular. Mostly funnelform. Corolla 5-lobed. Stamens 5. Spring and again in the fall.

Fruit   Consisting of 2 follicles each of which is about 2 inches or more in length.

Environment   Full sun or partial shade. Usually best in some shade, especially where hot. Tolerant to considerable shade. To below zero.

Pests   Root Knot Nematode

Propagation   Cuttings. Division.

Rate of Growth   Rapid

Pruning   Keep under control. Very aggressive. Spreads by rhizomes and stolons. Cut to soil level periodically.

Seasonal Value   Foliage. Flowers.

Shape   Upright. Forming a dense mat. Trailing.

Spread   Wide

Height   To 18 inches

Soil   Tolerant. But best with some moisture. Wilts when dry but recovers easily.

Use   Ground cover. Erosion control. Slopes.

Origin   Europe

Coments   Introduced to this country about 1789. It is used by the California Highway people for erosion control. There is a variegated form. *V. major 'Variegata'*.

Vinca minor

Family Apocynaceae

Leaves Evergreen. An herbaceous perennial. Opposite. Entire. Oblong to ovate. Glabrous and glandular-dotted both sides. Revolute. Dark, glossy green. 1 1/2 to 2 inches long. 1/2 to 3/4 inch across.

Flowers Lilac blue. About one inch across. Mostly funnelform. Solitary and axillary. About 1/2 inch across or more. Tube about 1/2 inch long, or less. Regular. Corolla 5-lobed. Stamens 5. Early spring and again in the fall.

Fruit A pair of erect or spreading 3-inch long follicles. Each with 6 to 8 seeds.

Environment Tolerant to full sun or partial shade. Usually best in some shade, where the foliage color is darker. Tolerant to considerable shade. To below zero.

Pests Root Knot Nematode

Propagation Cuttings. Division.

Rate of Growth Rapid

Pruning Keep under control. Aggressive. Spreading by stolons. Cut back to soil level periodically.

Seasonal Value Foliage. Flowers.

Shape Prostrate to mounding. Trailing.

Spread Wide

Height To 6 inches

Soil Tolerant, but usually best in a light, well-drained soil. Best with sufficient moisture.

Use Ground cover. Erosion control. Slopes. For shaded areas.

Origin Europe

Comments Usually better-appearing than *V. major* in the landscape. Effective for large areas where the soil is properly prepared. Thomas Jefferson is said to have planted it at his home in Monticello. There are various cultivars. These differ in having white, reddish, purple or blue flowers and even variegated foliage. These include 'Alba', 'Atropurpurea', 'Aureo-Variegata', 'Bowskii', 'Flore-Pleno' and 'Variegata'.

272

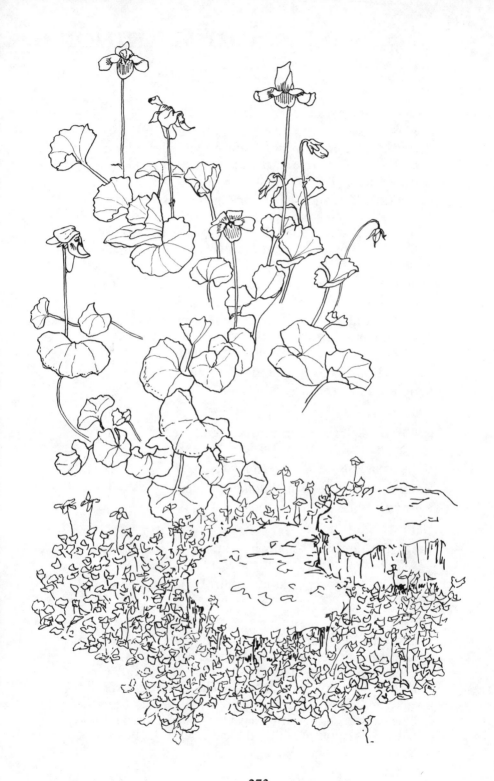

Viola hederacea

Family Violaceae

Leaves Evergreen. An herbaceous perennial. Alternate, basal or tufted. Crenate to nearly entire. Orbicular to reniform. Glabrous or pubescent. Glandular-dotted both sides. Medium green. 1/2 to 1 1/2 inches across. Nearly as long. With long petioles.

Flowers Usually blue. To 1/2 inch long. To 3/4 inch across. Solitary. Irregular. Petals 5. Stamens 5. Summer.

Fruit A 3-valved capsule.

Environment Full sun in coastal area. Partial shade where warm. From 20 to 30 degrees.

Pests Aphids. Mites.

Propagation Seed. Division.

Rate of Growth Moderate to rapid.

Pruning Keep under control. Aggressive. Spreading by stolons.

Seasonal Value Foliage. Flowers.

Shape Mat-forming

Spread 10 to 12 inches or more

Height 3 to 4 inches

Soil Fertile. Moist.

Use Ground cover. Between stepping stones. Best in small areas.

Origin Australia

Comments Formerly named *Erpetion reniforme*. The word *hederacea* means Ivy-like.

274

Viola odorata

Family Violaceae

Leaves Evergreen. An herbaceous perennial. Basal or tufted. Toothed. Cordate to ovate to reniform. Pubescent and glandular-dotted both sides. Ciliate. With bumps on upper side. Medium green. One to 2 inches long. Nearly as wide. With long petioles.

Flowers Violet. Rarely pink or white. To 3/4 inch across. Fragrant. Solitary. There are two kinds. In the spring the petals are showy. In the summer they are not and they are followed by fruit with abundant seed. Summer flowers are greenish and they are concealed below the foliage. They do not open and they are self pollinated. Irregular. Petals 5. Stamens 5.

Fruit A 3-valved capsule. To 3/4 inch across open. When the capsules pop open, the seed are scattered widely.

Environment Full sun or partial shade. Shade where hot. To below zero.

Pests Aphids. Mites.

Propagation Seed. Division.

Rate of Growth Rapid

Pruning Keep under control. Very aggressive. Spreading by long, rough stolons. Will naturalize.

Seasonal Value Foliage. Flowers. Fragrance (Flowers).

Shape Tufted. Stemless.

Spread Wide

Height 8 to 10 inches

Soil Fertile and moist.

Use Ground cover. Cut flowers. Used in floral industry.

Origin Africa. Asia. Europe.

Comments Is a source of perfume. There are many cultivars.

PLANT
CHARACTERISTICS

BOTANICAL CHARACTERISTICS

LEAVES

Aromatic

Achillea ageratifolia
Achillea tomentosa
Chamaemelum nobile
Cistus salvifolius
Galium odoratum
Gaultheria procumbens
Lantana montevidensis

Lavandula angustifolia 'Hidcote'
Mentha requienii
Rosmarinus officinalis 'Prostratus'
Santolina chamaecyparissus
Thymus praecox arcticus
Thymus pseudolanuginosus

Grasslike

Armeria maritima
Festuca ovina var. glauca

Ophiopogon japonicus
Pennisetum setaceum

Needlelike

Asparagus densiflorus 'Sprengeri'
Erica herbacea 'Springwood White'

Grevillea 'Noell'
Lotus berthelotii

Scalelike

Calluna vulgaris

Straplike

Agapanthus orientalis
Agapanthus orientalis 'Peter Pan'

Clivia miniata
Liriope muscari

Bluish-gray, Grayish or Whitish

Achillea ageratifolia
Achillea tomentosa
Andromeda polifolia 'Nana'*
Arabis caucasica
Arctotheca calendula
Armeria martima*

Aubrieta deltoidea
Aurinia saxatilis
Carpobrotus edulis*
Centranthus ruber
Cerastium tomentosum
Cistus salvifolius

279

Convolvulus cneorum
Convolvulus sabatius
Correa pulchella
Dianthus deltoides*
Drosanthemum floribundum
Festuca ovina var. glauca
Gazania 'Copper King'
Gazania rigens var. leucolaena
Gypsophila paniculata 'Pink Fairy'
Helianthemum nummularium 'Rose'
Hosta sieboldiana*
Hypericum coris
Lampranthus spectabilis

Lavandula angustifolia 'Hidcote'
Lithodora diffusa*
Lotus berthelotii
Phyla nodiflora*
Rosmarinus officinalis 'Prostratus'
Santolina chamaecyparissus
Saxifraga stolonifera*
Sedum brevifolium*
Senecio cineraria
Stachys byzantina
Thymus pseudolanuginosus
* Or green

Succulent

Carpobrotus edulis
Drosanthemum floribundum
Lampranthus spectabilis
Sedum acre

Sedum brevifolium
Sedum confusum
Sedum rubrotinctum

FLOWERS

Fragrant

Arabis caucasica
Asparagus densiflorus 'Sprengeri'
Centranthus ruber
Daphne cneorum
Dianthus deltoides
Gardenia augusta 'Radicans'
Lavandula angustifolia 'Hidcote'

Pachysandra terminalis
Pyracantha koidzumi 'Santa Cruz'
Rosmarinus officinalis 'Prostratus'
Sarcococca hookerana var. humilis
Trachelospermum jasminoides
Viola odorata

Irregular

Acanthus mollis
Ajuga reptans
Chorizema cordatum
Cymbalaria muralis
Glechoma hederacea

Grevillea 'Noell'
Justicia brandegeana
Lantana montevidensis
Laurentia fluviatilis
Lavandula angustifolia 'Hidcote'

280

Lotus berthelotii
Mentha requienii
Pratia angulata
Rosmarinus officinalis 'Prostratus'
Stachys byzantina
Thymus praecox arcticus

Thymus pseudolanuginosus
Verbena peruviana
Veronica repens
Viola hederacea
Viola odorata

Blue to Purplish

Acanthus mollis
Agapanthus orientalis
Agapanthus orientalis 'Peter Pan'
Ajuga reptans
Aubrieta deltoidea
Bergenia crassifolia
Calluna vulgaris
Campanula portenschlagiana
Campanula poscharskyana
Carpobrotus edulis
Ceratostigma plumbaginoides
Chorizema cordatum
Convolvulus sabatius
Cymbalaria muralis
Dianthus deltoides
Euonymus fortunei var. radicans
Felicia amelloides
Fuchsia procumbens
Geranium incanum
Glechoma hederacea
Grewia occidentalis
Hedyotis caerulea
Heterocentron elegans
Hosta sieboldiana
Justicia brandegeana

Lampranthus spectabilis
Lantana montevidensis
Laurentia fluviatilis
Lavandula angustifolia 'Hidcote'
Liriope muscari
Lithodora diffusa
Mentha requienii
Neirembergia hippomanica var. violace
Ophiopogon japonicus
Osteospermum fruticosum
Pelargonium peltatum
Pennisetum setaceum
Phlox subulata
Phyla nodiflora
Pratia angulata
Rosmarinus officinalis 'Prostratus'
Sollya heterophylla
Stachys byzantina
Thymus praecox arcticus
Verbena peruviana
Veronica repens
Vinca major
Vinca minor
Viola hederacea
Viola odorata

Pinkish

Acanthus mollis
Andromeda polifolia 'Nana'

Armeria maritima
Asparagus densiflorus 'Sprengeri'

Aubrieta deltoidea
Bergenia crassifolia
Calluna vulgaris
Carpobrotus edulis
Centranthus ruber
Convolvulus cneorum
Correa pulchella
Cotoneaster horizontalis
Cyclamen persicum
Daphne cneorum
Dianthus deltoides
Drosanthemum floribundum
Erodium chamaedryoides
Francoa ramosa
Gaultheria procumbens
Geranium incanum
Grevillea 'Noell'
Grewia occidentalis
Gypsophila paniculata 'Pink Fairy'
Helianthemum nummularium 'Rose'

Heuchera sanguinea
Lampranthus spectabilis
Lantana montevidensis
Myoporum parvifolium
Pachysandra terminalis
Pelargonium peltatum
Pennisetum setaceum
Pernettya mucronata
Phlox subulata
Phyla nodiflora
Polygonum capitatum
Prunus laurocerasus 'Zabeliana'
Saxifraga stolonifera
Sedum brevifolium
Soleirolia soleirolii
Thymus pseudolanuginosus
Trachelospermum jasminoides
Tradescantia albiflora
Verbena peruviana
Viola odorata

Reddish

Aubrieta deltoidea
Centranthus ruber
Clivia miniata
Cyclamen persicum
Gazania 'Copper King'
Helianthemum nummularium 'Rose'
Heterocentron elegans

Heuchera sanguinea
Lampranthus spectabilis
Lotus berthelotii
Pelargonium peltatum
Phlox subulata
Sedum rubrotinctum
Verbena peruviana

Yellow to Orange

Achillea tomentosa
Arctotheca calendula
Aurinia saxatilis
Berberis stenophylla 'Irwinii'
Carpobrotus edulis
Chamaemelum nobile

Chorizema cordatum
Clivia miniata
Coreopsis auriculata 'Nana'
Dichondra micrantha
Duchesnea indica
Erysimum kotschyanum

Fuchsia procumbens
Gazania 'Copper King'
Gazania rigens var. leucolaena
Helianthemum nummularium 'Rose'
Hypericum calycinum
Hypericum coris
Lysimachia nummularia

Potentilla tabernaemontanii
Santolina chamaecyparissus
Sedum acre
Sedum confusum
Sedum rubrotinctum
Senecio cineraria

Whitish

Acanthus mollis
Achillea ageratifolia
Agapanthus orientalis
Agapanthus orientalis 'Peter Pan'
Arabis caucasica
Ardisia japonica
Armeria maritima
Asparagus densiflorus 'Sprengeri'
Calluna vulgaris
Cerastium tomentosum
Chlorophytum comosum
Cistus salvifolius
Convolvulus cneorum
Coprosma kirkii
Cotoneaster dammeri
Cotoneaster horizontalis
Cotoneaster microphyllus
Cyclamen persicum
Daphne cneorum
Dianthus deltoides
Erica herbacea 'Springwood White'
Erigeron karvinskianus
Erodium chamaedryoides
Euonymus fortunei var. radicans
Francoa ramosa
Galium odoratum
Gardenia augusta 'Radicans'

Gaultheria procumbens
Gazania rigens var. leucolaena
Grevillea 'Noell'
Gypsophila paniculata 'Pink Fairy'
Hedyotis caerulea
Helianthemum nummularium 'Rose'
Herniaria glabra
Iberis sempervirens
Justicia brandegeana
Loropetalum chinense
Myoporum parvifolium
Osteospermum fruticosum
Pachysandra terminalis
Pelargonium peltatum
Pernettya mucronata
Phlox subulata
Pratia angulata
Prunus laurocerasus 'Zabeliana'
Pyracantha koidzumi 'Santa Cruz'
Sagina subulata 'Aurea'
Sarcococca hookerana var. humilis
Saxifraga stolonifera
Sedum brevifolium
Soleirolia soleirolii
Thymus praecox arcticus
Thymus pseudolanuginosus
Trachelospermum jasminoides

Tradescantia albiflora
Verbena peruviana
Veronica repens
Viburnum davidii

Vinca major
Vinca minor
Viola hederacea
Viola odorata

Spring - Flowering

Acanthus mollis
Achillea ageratifolila
Ajuga reptans
Andromeda polifolia 'Nana'
Arabis caucasica
Arctotheca calendula
Armeria maritima
Asparagus densiflorus 'Sprengeri'
Aubrieta deltoidea
Aurinia saxatilis
Berberis stenophylla 'Irwinii'
Bergenia crassifolia
Campanula poscharskyana
Carpobrotus edulis
Centranthus ruber
Chorizema cordatum
Cistus salvifolius
Clivia miniata
Coprosma kirkii
Coreopsis auriculata 'Nana'
Correa pulchella
Cotoneaster dammeri
Cotoneaster horizontalis
Cotoneaster microphyllus
Cyclamen persicum
Daphne cneorum
Dianthus deltoides
Drosanthemum floribundum
Duchesnea indica
Erica herbacea 'Springwood White'
Erigeron karvinskianus

Erodium chanaedryoides
Erysimum kotschyanum
Galium odoratum
Gazania 'Copper King'
Gazania rigens var. leucolaena
Geranium incanum
Glechoma hederacea
Grevillea 'Noell'
Grewia occidentalis
Hedyotis caerulea
Helianthemum nummularium 'Rose'
Heuchera sanguinea
Hosta sieboldiana
Hypericum calycinum
Hypericum coris
Iberis sempervirens
Lampranthus spectabilis
Lantana montevidensis
Laurentia fluviatilis
Lithodora diffusa
Loropetalum chinense
Osteospermum fruticosum
Pachysandra terminalis
Pelargonium peltatum
Pernettya mucronata
Phlox subulata
Phyla nodiflora
Polygonum capitatum
Potentilla tabernaemontanii
Pratia angulata
Prunus laurocerasus 'Zabeliana'

Pyracantha koidzumi 'Santa Cruz'
Rosmarinus officinalis 'Prostratus'
Saxifraga stolonifera
Sedum acre
Sedum brevifolium
Sedum confusum

Sedum rubrotinctum
Thymus pseudolanuginosus
Veronica repens
Vinca major
Vinca minor
Viola odorata

Summer - Flowering

Acanthus mollis
Achillea ageratifolia
Achillea tomentosa
Agapanthus orientalis
Agapanthus orientalis 'Peter Pan'
Ajuga reptans
Arctotheca calendula
Armeria maritima
Asparagus densiflorus 'Sprengeri'
Aurinia saxatilis
Bergenia crassifolia
Calluna vulgaris
Campanula portenschlagiana
Campanula poseharskyana
Carpobrotus edulis
Centranthus ruber
Cerastium tomentosum
Ceratostigma plumbaginoides
Chamaemelum nobile
Chorizema cordatum
Convolvulus cneorum
Convolvulus sabatius
Coreopsis auriculata 'Nana'
Cotoneaster dammeri
Cotoneaster horizontalis
Cotoneaster microphyllus
Cymbalaria muralis
Dianthus deltoides
Drosanthemum floribundum

Duchesnea indica
Erigeron karvinskianus
Erodium chamaedryoides
Erysimum kotschyanum
Euonymus fortunei var. radicans
Felicia amelloides
Festuca ovina var. glauca
Francoa ramosa
Fuchsia procumbens
Galium odoratum
Gardenia augusta 'Radicans'
Gaultheria procumbens
Gazania 'Copper King'
Gazania rigens var. leucolaena
Geranium incanum
Glechoma hederacea
Grewia occidentalis
Gypsophila paniculata 'Pink Fairy'
Hedyotis caerulea
Helianthemum nummularium 'Rose
Heterocentron elegans
Heuchera sanguinea
Hosta sieboldiana
Hypericum calycinum
Hypericum coris
Iberis sempervirens
Justicia brandegeana
Lantana montevidensis
Laurentia fluviatilis

Lavandula angustifolia 'Hidcote'
Liriope muscari
Lithodora diffusa
Lotus berthelotii
Lysimachia nummularia
Mentha requienii
Myoporum parvifolium
Nierembergia hippomanica var. violacea
Ophiopogon japonicus
Osteospermum fruticosum
Pachysandra terminalis
Pelargonium peltatum
Pernettya mucronata
Phlox subulata
Phyla nodiflora
Polygonum capitatum
Potentilla tabernaemontanii
Pratia angulata

Prunus laurocerasus 'Zabeliana'
Rosmarinus officinalis 'Prostratus'
Sagina subulata 'Aurea'
Santolina chamaecyparissus
Saxifraga stolonifera
Sedum acre
Sedum brevifolium
Sedum confusum
Sedum rubrotinctum
Senecio cineraria
Sollya heterophylla
Stachys byzantina
Thymus praecox arcticus
Trachelospermum jasminoides
Tradescantia albiflora
Verbena peruviana
Viburnum davidii
Viola hederacea

Fall - Flowering

Achillea ageratifolia
Achillea tomentosa
Agapanthus orientalis
Agapanthus orientalis 'Peter Pan'
Ajuga reptans
Arctotheca calendula
Ardisia japonica
Armeria maritima
Asparagus densiflorus 'Sprengeri'
Calluna vulgaris
Campanula portenschlagiana
Campanula poscharskyana
Centranthus ruber
Ceratostigma plumbaginoides
Chlorophytum comosum
Clivia miniata
Convolvulus cneorum

Convolvulus sabatius
Coreopsis auriculata 'Nana'
Correa pulchella
Cyclamen persicum
Cymbalaria muralis
Dianthus deltoides
Duchesnea indica
Erigeron karvinskianus
Erodium chamaedryoides
Felicia amelloides
Fuchsia procumbens
Gaultheria procumbens
Geranium incanum
Grewia occidentalis
Gypsophila paniculata 'Pink Fairy'
Hedera canariensis
Hedera helix

Hedera helix 'Hahn's Self-Branching'
Heuchera sanguinea
Lantana montevidensis
Lysimachia nummularia
Osteospermum fruticosum
Pelargonium peltatum
Phyla nodiflora

Polygonum capitatum
Rosmarinus officinalis 'Prostratus'
Sarcococca hookerana var. humilis
Thymus praecox arcticus
Tradescantia albiflora
Vinca major
Vinca minor

Winter - Flowering

Bergenia crassifolia
Clivia miniata
Correa pulchella
Cyclamen persicum
Duchesnea indica
Erica herbacea 'Springwood White'
Erigeron karvinskianus

Iberis sempervirens
Lantana montevidensis
Osteospermum fruticosum
Polygonum capitatum
Rosmarinus officinalis 'Prostratus'
Sarcococca hookerana var. humilis

FRUIT

Blue, Purplish or Black

Berberis stenophylla 'Irwinii'
Grewia occidentalis
Hedera canariensis
Hedera helix
Hedera helix 'Hahn's Self-Branching'
Liriope muscari
Myoporum parvifolium

Ophipogon japonicus
Pernettya mucronata
Pratia angulata
Prunus laurocerasus 'Zabeliana'
Sarcococca hookerana var. humilis
Sollya heterophyllus
Viburnum davidii

Reddish

Ardisia japonica
Asparagus densiflorus 'Sprengeri'
Clivia miniata
Cotoneaster dammeri

Cotoneaster horizontalis
Cotoneaster microphyllus
Duchesnea indica
Fuchsia procumbens

Gaultheria procumbens
Grewia occidentalis
Pernettya mucronata

Pratia angulata
Pyracantha koidzumi 'Santa Cruz'

White .
Pachysandra terminalis

Pernettya mucronata

GROUND COVERS
FOR
PARTICULAR USES
OR SITUATIONS

Drought-Tolerant *

Achillea ageratifolia
Achillea tomentosa
Agapanthus orientalis
Agapanthus orientalis 'Peter Pan'
Arabis caucasica
Arctotheca calendula
Armeria maritima
Aubrieta deltoidea
Aurinia saxatilis
Calluna vulgaris
Carpobrotus edulis
Centranthus ruber
Cerastium tomentosum
Chamaemelum nobile
Chorizema cordatum
Cistus salvifolius
Convolvulus cneorum
Convolvulus sabatius
Coprosma kirkii
Coreopsis auriculata 'Nana'
Correa pulchella
Cotoneaster dammeri
Cotoneaster horizontalis
Cotoneaster microphyllus
Dianthus deltoides
Drosanthemum floribundum
Erica herbacea 'Springwood White'
Erigeron karvinskianus
Erysimum kotschyanum
Euonymus fortunei var. radicans
Felicia amelloides
Festuca ovina var. glauca
Gazania 'Copper King'
Gazania rigens var. leucolaena
Grevillea 'Noell'
Gypsophila paniculata 'Pink Fairy'
Hedera canariensis
Hedera helix

Hedera helix 'Hahn's Self-Branching'
Helianthemum nummularium 'Rose'
Heterocentron elegans
Hypericum calycinum
Hypericum coris
Iberis sempervirens
Lampranthus spectabilis
Lantana montevidensis
Lavandula angustifolia 'Hidcote'
Lithodora diffusa
Lotus berthelotii
Myoporum parvifolium
Nierembergia hippomanica var. violacea
Ophiopogon japonicus
Osteospermum fruticosum
Pelargonium peltatum
Pennisetum setaceum
Phlox subulata
Phyla nodiflora
Polygonum capitatum
Potentilla tabernaemontanii
Prunus laurocerasus 'Zabeliana'
Pyracantha koidzumi 'Santa Cruz'
Rosmarinus officinalis 'Prostratus'
Santolina chamaecyparissus
Sedum acre
Sedum brevifolium
Sedum confusum
Sedum rubrotinctum
Senecio cineraria
Sollya heterophylla
Stachys byzantina
Thymus praecox arcticus
Thymus pseudolanuginosus
Verbena peruviana
Vinca major
Vinca minor

* Most plants will look better with sufficient water.

Dye Plants *

Achillea
Berberis
Campanula
Chamaemelum
Cistus
Convolvulus
Coreopsis
Daphne
Erica
Erodium
Erysimum
Euonymus
Galium
Geranium
Glechoma
Grevillea
Grewia

Heuchera
Hypericum
Lysimachia
Mentha
Pelargonium
Polygonum
Potentilla
Prunus
Rosmarinus
Santolina
Sedum
Senecio
Stachys
Verbena
Viburnum
Viola

* Various species of the above have been used.

Edible Plants *

Achillea
Asparagus
Calluna
Carpobrotus
Chamaemelum
Cymbalaria
Dianthus
Galium
Gaultheria
Glechoma

Mentha
Pelargonium
Polygonum
Prunus
Pyracantha
Rosmarinus
Stachys
Thymus
Veronica

* Parts of various species of these plants have been used.

Note: Correctly identify before using for food!

Erosion Control

Arctotheca calendula
Asparagus densiflorus 'Sprengeri'

Cistus salvifolius
Convolvulus sabatius

292

Coprosma kirkii
Correa pulchella
Cotoneaster dammeri
Cotoneaster horizontalis
Cotoneaster microphyllus
Drosanthemum floribundum
Euonymus fortunei var. radicans
Gazania 'Copper King'
Gazania rigens var. leucolaena
Hedera canariensis
Hedera helix
Hedera helix 'Hahn's Self-Branching'
Hypericum calycinum
Lampranthus spectabilis

Lantana montevidensis
Lotus berthelotii
Myoporum parvifolium
Ophiopogon japonicus
Osteospermum fruticosum
Pelargonium peltatum
Polygonum capitatum
Pyracantha koidzumi 'Santa Cruz'
Rosmarinus officinalis 'Prostratus'
Trachelospermum jasminoides
Verbena peruviana
Vinca major
Vinca minor

Fire - Resistant *

Achillea tomentosa
Carpobrotus edulis
Convolvulus cneorum
Drosanthemum floribundum
Gazania 'Copper King'
Gazania rigens var. leucolaena
Lampranthus spectabilis

Myoporum parvifolium
Rosmarinus officinalis 'Prostratus'
Sedum acre
Sedum brevifolium
Sedum confusum
Sedum rubrotinctum
Senecio cineraria

*These plants are said to be fire-resistant, but only when they are irrigated periodically.

Hanging Baskets

Asparagus densiflorus 'Sprengeri'
Campanula portenschlagiana
Campanula poscharskyana
Chlorophytum comosum
Cymbalaria muralis
Drosanthemum floribundum
Erigeron karvinskianus
Fuchsia procumbens
Gazania rigens var. leucolaena
Glechoma hederacea
Hedera helix
Hedera helix 'Hahn's Self-Branching'
Helianthemum nummularium

Heterocentron elegans
Lampranthus spectabilis
Lantana montevidensis
Lithodora diffusa
Lotus berthelotii
Lysimachia nummularia
Myoporum parvifolium
Osteospermum fruticosum
Pelargonium peltatum
Polygonum capitatum
Saxifraga stolonifera
Sedum rubrotinctum
Tradescantia albiflora

INDOOR USE

Cut Flowers

Acanthus mollis
Agapanthus orientalis
Agapanthus orientalis 'Peter Pan'
Centranthus ruber
Dianthus deltoides
Felicia amelloides

Francoa ramosa
Gypsophila paniculata 'Pink Fairy'
Heuchera sanguinea
Iberis sempervirens
Lavandula angustifolia 'Hidcote'

Dried Arrangements

Acanthus mollis
Achillea tomentosa
Festuca ovina var. glauca
Hosta sieboldiana (Foliage)

Lavandula angustifolia 'Hidcote'
Pennisetum setaceum
Santolina chamaecyparissus

Hanging Baskets

Asparagus densiflorus 'Sprengeri'
Chlorophytum comosum
Cymbalaria muralis
Drosanthemum floribundum
Hedera helix

Hedera helix 'Hahn's Self-Branching'
Lampranthus spectabilis
Saxifraga stolonifera
Sedum rubrotinctum
Tradescantia albiflora

Planters

Acanthus mollis
Agapanthus orientalis 'Peter Pan'
Asparagus densiflorus 'Sprengeri'
Chlorophytum comosum
Clivia miniata
Cyclamen persicum
Hedera helix
Hedera helix 'Hahn's Self-Branching'

Liriope muscari
Ophiopogon japonicus
Saxifraga stolonifera
Sedum acre
Sedum brevifolium
Sedum confusum
Sedum rubrotinctum
Tradescantia albiflora

Tolerant to Seacoast Conditions

Achillea ageratifolia
Achillea tomentosa
Arctotheca calendula
Armeria maritima

Aurinia saxatilis
Bergenia crassifolia
Calluna vulgaris
Campanula portenschlagiana

Campanula poscharskyana
Carpobrotus edulis
Cerastium tomentosum
Cistus salvifolius
Coprosma kirkii
Cotoneaster dammeri
Cotoneaster horizontalis
Cotoneaster microphyllus
Drosanthemum floribundum
Erica herbacea 'Springwood White'
Felicia amelloides
Festuca ovina var. glauca
Galium odoratum
Helianthemum nummularium
Hypericum calycinum
Hypericum coris

Iberis sempervirens
Lampranthus spectabilis
Lantana montevidensis
Lavandula angustifolia 'Hidcote'
Liriope muscari
Muehlenbeckia axillaris
Osteospermum fruticosum
Potentilla tabernaemontanii
Rosmarinus officinalis 'Prostratus'
Sagina subulata 'Aurea'
Santolina chamaecyparissus
Thymus praecox arcticus
Thymus pseudolanuginosus
Verbena peruviana
Veronica repens

Usually Best in Partial Shade

Acanthus mollis
Agapanthus orientalis
Agapanthus orientalis 'Peter Pan'
Ajuga reptans
Ardisia japonica
Asparagus densiflorus 'Sprengeri'
Bergenia crassifolia
Campanula portenschlagiana
Campanula poscharskyana
Chlorophytum comosum
Clivia miniata
Cyclamen persicum
Cymbalaria muralis
Dichondra micrantha
Duchesnea indica
Francoa ramosa
Fuchsia procumbens
Galium odoratum
Gaultheria procumbens
Glechoma hederacea
Hedyotis caerulea

Herniaria glabra
Heterocentron elegans
Hosta sieboldiana
Justicia brandegeana
Laurentia fluviatilis
Liriope muscari
Lysimachia nummularia
Mentha requienii
Ophiopogon japonicus
Pachysandra terminalis
Pratia angulata
Prunus laurocerasus 'Zabeliana'
Sagina subulata 'Aurea'
Sarococcoca hookerana var. humilis
Saxifraga stolonifera
Soleirolia soleirolii
Sollya heterophylla
Tradescantia albiflora
Viburnum davidii
Vinca major
Vinca minor

Tolerant to Considerable Shade

Acanthus mollis
Agapanthus orientalis 'Peter Pan'
Ajuga reptans
Chlorophytum comosum
Clivia miniata
Dichondra micrantha
Euonymus fortunei var. radicans
Francoa ramosa
Glechoma hederacea
Hedera canariensis
Hedera helix

Hedera helix 'Hahn's Self-Branching'
Heterocentron elegans
Hosta sieboldiana
Liriope muscari
Ophiopogon japonicus
Pachysandra terminalis
Sarcococca hookerana var. humilis
Soleirolia soleirolii
Tradescantia albiflora
Vinca major
Vinca minor

Usually Best in Full Sun

Achillea ageratifolia
Achillea tomentosa
Arabis caucasica
Arctotheca calendula
Armeria maritima
Aubrieta deltoidea
Aurinia saxatilis
Calluna vulgaris
Carpobrotus edulis
Cerastium tomentosum
Chamaemelum nobile
Cistus salvifolius
Convolvulus cneorum
Convolvulus sabatius
Coreopsis auriculata 'Nana'
Cotoneaster dammeri
Cotoneaster horizontalis
Cotoneaster microphyllus
Daphne cneorum
Dianthus deltoides
Drosanthemum floribundum
Erica herbacea ''Springwood White'
Erysimum kotschyanum
Felicia amelloides
Festuca ovina var. glauca
Gardenia augusta 'Radicans'
Gazania 'Copper King'
Gazania rigens var. leucolaena

Geranium incanum
Grevillea 'Noell'
Grewia occidentalis
Gypsophilia paniculata 'Pink Fairy'
Helianthemum nummularium 'Rose'
Hypericum calycinum
Hypericum coris
Iberis sempervirens
Lampranthus spectabilis
Lantana montevidensis
Lavandula angustifolia 'Hidcote'
Lithodora diffusa
Lotus berthelotii
Myoporum parvifolium
Nierembergia hippomanica
  var. violacea
Osteospermum fruticosum
Pelargonium peltatum
Pernettya mucronata
Phlox subulata
Phyla nodiflora
Polygonum capitatum
Pyracantha koidzumi 'Santa Cruz'
Rosmarinus officinalis 'Prostratus'
Santolina chamaecyparissus
Senecio cineraria
Stachys byzantina
Verbena peruviana

Between Stepping Stones

Achillea tomentosa
Ajuga reptans
Arabis caucasica
Armeria maritima
Aubrieta deltoidea
Campanula portenschlagiana
Cerastium tomentosum
Chamaemelum nobile
Cymbalaria muralis
Dianthus deltoides
Hedyotis caerulea
Lysimachia nummularia

Mentha requienii
Muehlenbeckia axillaris
Ophiopogon japonicus
Phlox subulata
Sagina subulata 'Aurea'
Saxifraga stolonifera
Sedum acre
Sedum brevifolium
Soleirolia soleirolii
Thymus praecox arcticus
Thymus pseudolanuginosus
Veronica repens

BIBLIOGRAPHY

Amfac. *Ground Cover Guide.* American Garden Perrys. 1979

Bailey, L.H. *The Standard Cyclopedia of Horticulture.* The MacMillan Company. New York, N.Y. 1939

Bailey, L.H. *How Plants Get Their Names.* Dover Publications, Inc. New York, N.Y. 1963

Bailey, L.H. *Manual of Cultivated Plants.* The MacMillan Company. New York, N.Y. 1949

Bailey and Bailey. *Hortus Third.* Ibid. 1976

Clarke, C.B. *Edible and Useful Plants of California.* University of California Press. Berkeley, CA. 1977

Conner, E. Wesley. *The Back Pocket Guide to Ornamental Plants.* Vocational Education Productions. California State Polytechnic University, San Luis Obispo, California. 1976

Courtright, Gordon. *Trees and Shrubs for Western Gardens.* Timber Press. Forest Grove, Ore. 1979

Essig, E.O. *Insects of Western North America.* MacMillan Publishing Company, Inc. New York, N.Y. 1947

Fisher, Satchell and Watkins. *Gardening with New Zealand Plants, Shrubs and Trees.* Collins Bros. & Co. Ltd. Auckland, N.Z. 1971

Foley, Daniel J. *Ground Covers for Easier Gardening.* Dover Publications, Inc. New York, N.Y. 1972

Grae, Ida. *Natures Colors. Dyes from Plants.* Collier Books. The MacMillan Publishing Co., Inc. New York, N.Y. 1979

Harrington and Durrell. *How to Identify Plants.* The Swallow Press, Inc. Chicago, Ill. 1957

Hedrick, E.P. *Sturtevants Edible Plants of the World.* Dover Publications. New York, N.Y. 1972

King. E.A. *Bible Plants for American Gardens.* Ibid. 1975

Mathias, Mildred E. *Color for the Landscape.* California Arboretum Foundation, Inc. Arcadia, CA 1976

McClintock and Leiser. *An Annotated Checklist of Woody Ornamental Plants of California, Oregon and Washington.* Division of Agricultural Sciences. University of California. Berkeley, CA 1979

Mondodori, Arnoldi. *Complete Guide to Plants and Flowers.* Simon and Schuster. New York, N.Y. 1979

Muenscher, W.C. *Poisonous Plants of the United States.* The MacMillan Publishing Co., Inc., New York, N.Y. 1962

Nehrling, Arno and Irene. *Easy Gardening with Drought-Resistant Plants.* Hearthside Press, Inc., New York, N.Y. 1968

Ortho Books. *All About Ground Covers.* Chevron Chemical Co. Ortho Division. San Francisco, CA 1977

Pirone, Pascal P. *Diseases and Pests of Ornamental Plants.* John Wiley and Sons. New York, N.Y. 1978

Salmon, J.T. *New Zealand Flowers and Plants in Colour.* A.H. & A.W. Reed Ltd. Wellington 3, New Zealand. 1982

Sunset. *Lawns and Ground Covers.* Lane Book Company. Menlo Park, CA 1981

Sunset. *New Western Garden Book.* Ibid. 1979

Wyman, Donald. *Ground Cover Plants.* The MacMillan Publishing Co. Inc., New York, N.Y. 1964

Glossary

Acerose - *Needlelike*
Achene - *A small, dry, one-celled, one-seeded indehiscent fruit*
Acicular - *See acerose*
Acuminate - *Tapering to the apex, with the sides pinched in*
Acute - *Tapering to the apex, with the sides about straight*
Aggregate - *A cluster of small fruit, developing from one flower*
Alternate - *With one leaf at a node*
Annual - *Life cycle completed in one season*
Apex - *The tip*
Auricle - *An ear-shaped lobe or appendage*
Auriculate - *With auricles*
Awl-shaped - *Tapering to a point; marrowly triangular*
Axillary - *Borne in an axil of a leaf*

Berry - *A fleshy, few to many-seeded fruit, with immersed seed*
Bisexual - *Having both stamens and pistils; perfect*
Blade - *The flat part of a leaf or petal*
Bloom - *The whitish, powdery covering of a surface; glaucous*
Bract - *A small leaflike structure near a flower or inflorescence*

Calyx - *The outer portion of the flower; sepals*
Campanulate - *Bell-shaped*
Capsule - *A dry fruit; dehiscent, and usually with more than one seed*
Carpel - *The female structure bearing the ovules; an ovary consists of one or more carpels*
Chlorotic - *Not having a normal green color*
Ciliate - *With a marginal fringe of hairs*
Cladode - *A flattened stem, with the form and function of a leaf, but arising from the axil of a tiny, bractlike leaf*
Cleft - *Cut in about one-half way to the midvein or to the base*
Complete - *A flower that has sepals, petals, stamens and pistils*
Compound - *Consisting of two or more distinct segments*

301

Cordate - *Heart-shaped; widest at the base*
Coriaceous - *Leathery*
Corolla - *Composed of the petals*
Corymb - *A racemelike inflorescence which is flat or convex at the top*
Crenate - *With rounded teeth*
Crown - *Referring to the base of a plant at the soil line*
Cultivar - *A plant variation developed by human effort*
Cuneate - *Wedge-shaped; narrowest the base*
Cuspidate - *With a short, sharp, firm point*
Cyme - *An inflorescence where the terminal flower blooms first*

Deciduous - *Leaves all dying and falling off, usually in the winter period*
Decurrent - *Extending downward from the point of insertion*
Decussate - *In opposite pairs, alternately arranged at right angles, to form four vertical rows along an axis*
Dehiscent - *Splitting open at maturity*
Deltoid - *Triangular shape; broadest at the base*
Dentate - *Teeth are directed outward and are usually coarse*
Dioecious - *Male and female flowers on separate plants*
Dissected - *Divided into numerous, usually narrow segments*
Divided - *Deeply lobed; nearly compound*
Drupe - *A fleshy, indehiscent, one-seeded fruit*

Elliptic - *Widest in the center, with the two ends equal*
Emarginate - *Shallowly notched at the apex*
Endemic - *Confined to a limited geographical area*
Entire - *Margins not toothed*
Evergreen - *With green leaves all year round*
Exotic - *Not native; introduced*

Falcate - *Asymmetric; curved sideways; tapering to an apex*
Fascicled - *In close clusters or bundles*
Follicle - *A dry fruit with one carpel; splitting down one side only*
Funnelform - *As a funnel, with the wider part upward*

Gamopetalous - *With petals more or less united*
Glabrous - *With no hairs*
Glaucous - *Covered with a whitish, grayish or bluish waxy bloom*

Globose - *Round, as a globe*

Hastate - *Arrow-shaped, with basal lobes pointing outward*
Head - *A short, dense spike; compositae.*
Head (In pruning) - *Cutting to buds or to a weak lateral;
            often leaving an unnatural-looking plant*
Herbaceous - *With no persistent woody stem above ground*
Hybrid - *A cross between two related species*

Imbricated - *Overlapping, as the shingles on a roof*
Indehiscent - *Not splitting open*
Indigenous - *Native to an area*
Inflorescence - *Arrangement of flowers on a stem*
Involucre - *A whorl of leaves or bracts subtending a flower
            or an inflorescence*
Involute - *With margins rolled upward*
Irregular - *Not symmetrical*

Lanceolate - *Lance-shaped; widest below the middle*
Leaflet - *A division of a compound leaf*
Legume - *A pod; the fruit of a member of the
            Leguminosae family*
Linear - *Long and narrow, with parallel sides*
Lobe - *A division of a leaf, especially if rounded*
Lyrate - *Pinnatifid; with a large and rounded terminal lobe
            and with the lower lobes being small*

Midrib - *Main or central vein of a leaf*
Midvein - *See Midrib*
Monoecious - *Male and female flowers on the same plant*
Mucronate - *With a small, toothlike apex; not especially
            sharp*

Nerve - *A simple or unbranched vein*
Node - *Place on a stem where a leaf is attached*
Nut - *A dry, hard, one-celled, indehiscent fruit*

Obcordate - *Inversely cordate*
Oblanceolate - *Inversely lanceolate*
Oblique - *With sides unequal, especially at the base*
Oblong - *With parallel sides and two to four times longer
            than wide*
Obovate - *Inversely ovate*
Obovoid - *Inversely ovoid*
Obtuse - *Blunt to rounded at the apex*
Opposite - *With two leaves at a node*

Orbicular - *Circular; a leaf that is rounded*
Ovate - *Egg-shaped; widest at the base; an ovate leaf*
Ovoid - *Egg-shaped; as an egg*

Palmately compound - *With all the leaflets borne at the top of the petiole*
Panicle - *A compound flower cluster with the younger flowers at the center*
Pappilae - *Minute, pimplelike protuberances*
Pappus - *In Compositae - the modified calyx limb forming a plumose, bristlelike or other type crown*
Parted - *Lobed, or cut in over half-way to base of midrib*
Pedicel - *Stalk of a single flower of an inflorescence*
Peduncle - *Stalk of a single flower or of an inflorescence*
Peltate - *With the petiole attached to the leaf blade in from the margin*
Pendulous - *Weeping; hanging down*
Perennial - *Living for three or more years*
Perianth - *Consisting of the calyx and the corolla, especially when they cannot be distinguished*
Petiole - *Stalk to a leaf blade or to a compound leaf*
Pinna - *One of the primary divisions of a pinnately compound leaf*
Pinnately compound - *With the leaflets on opposite sides of an axis*
Pistillate - *Female; comprised of pistils*
Pod - *Legume; a dry, dehiscent fruit of the Leguminosae family*
Polygamous - *With both dioecious and monoecious flowers, either on the same plant, or on separate plants*
Procumbent - *Lying or trailing on the soil surface but usually not rooting at the nodes*
Pubescent - *With short, soft hairs*

Raceme - *A compound flower cluster with the flower stems of equal length and with the younger flowers nearest the apex*
Receptacle - *The somewhat expanded part of the flower stalk which bears the flower organs*
Regular - *Radially symmetrical*
Reniform - *Kidney-shaped*
Repand - *See undulate*
Reticulate - *In the form of a network*

Revolute - *Rolled downward from the margins*
Rhizome - *A horizontal, underground stem*
Rhombic - *Diamond-shaped; in the form of a rhomboid,
          with the opposite sides parallel*
Rugose - *With a wrinkled surface*

Samara - *A dry, indehiscent, winged fruit*
Sagittate - *Arrow-shaped, with the basal lobes directed
            backwards*
Scabrous - *Rough to the touch*
Scurfy - *Covered with small, scalelike particles*
Serrate - *With the sharp teeth directed forward*
Serrulate - *Finely serrate*
Sessile - *Without a stalk*
Silicle - *A short fruit of a plant in the Cruciferae family;
          usually not more than twice as long as wide*
Silique - *Also a fruit of the Cruciferae family; elongated
          and longer than a silicle*
Simple - *Consisting of one part*
Sinus - *The area between two adjoining lobes*
Spatulate - *Spoon-shaped; broad and rounded at the apex*
Spike - *A compound flower cluster with sessile flowers on
        an elongated axis, and with the younger
        flowers at the apex*
Spine - *A strong, sharp-pointed woody outgrowth from the
        stem*
Spinose - *Bearing spines*
Staminate - *Male; with stamens*
Stellate - *Starlike; starshaped*
Sterile - *Infertile and unproductive*
Stipulate - *With stipules*
Stipule - *An appendage at the base of a petiole or leaf*
Stolon - *A horizontal, above-ground stem*
Stomata - *Small openings in the leaf surface*
Strigose - *With appressed, stiff, short hairs*
Subulate - *Awl-shaped. Narrowly triangular*
Succulent - *Fleshy and with juice*

Terete - *Circular in outline and more or less elongated*
Thin (In pruning) - *Cutting to laterals or to the main trunk,
          so as to leave a natural-appearing plant*
Tomentose - *With hairs closely interwoven*
Truncate - *Squared at the apex or the base*

Umbel - *A compound flower cluster with the flowers all from one point and with the younger flowers in the center*

Undulated - *With a wavy margin*

Urceolate - *Urn-shaped*

Utricle - *A small fruit that is as a bladder; thin-walled and one-seeded*

Valve - *One of the parts into which a deshiscent fruit splits*

Verticillaster - *An inflorescence where the flowers seem to be in a whorl, but composed of a pair of dense, opposite cymes in the axils of opposite leaves; in the Labiatae family*

Viscid - Sticky

Whorled - *With three or more parts from one point*

Woody - *With an above-ground persistent woody stem or trunk*

INDEX

308

Emile L. Labadie

A native of San Francisco, Emile Labadie has an A.B. from the University of California at Berkeley, a B.S. from California State Polytechnic University at San Luis Obispo and an M.S. from the University of California at Davis.

With the San Mateo County Department of Agriculture for many years, Labadie left his position as Deputy Agricultural Commissioner to develop a Horticulture Program at Merritt College in Oakland.

For his achievements in horticultural education, he received awards from the California Association of Nurserymen and the Northern California Turfgrass Council.

After 30 years in horticulture, and with the program at Merritt well-established, he retired in 1977, to become a private Horticultural Consultant.

Jane Stevens Andrews

Born in Long Island, New York, Jane Andrews received her B.F.A. from Drake University in Iowa.

After winning several awards for her art work in the East, she moved to California, to teach for many years in the Richmond Unified School District.

Leaving this area of education, she enrolled in and completed the Horticulture Program at Merritt College. She now teaches courses there as a part-time instructor. She is loved and respected by her students.

Besides being a botanical illustrator, Andrews continues to express herself as a talented artist. Her beautiful illustrations reflect her devotion to detail and to botanical accuracy.